COPING WITH LIFE

HUGH O. DOUGLAS

COPING WITH LIFE

Foreword by
LORD MACLEOD of FUINARY

Published by
ARTHUR JAMES LIMITED
ONE CRANBOURNE ROAD, LONDON N10 2BT

First published 1964
Paperback Edition 1988

© *Hugh O. Douglas 1964*

All rights reserved by
Arthur James Limited of London, England

ISBN 85305 282 4

Printed and bound in Great Britain by
The Guernsey Press Co. Ltd., Guernsey, Channel Islands

To
my wife, Isabel
for coping with me.

ACKNOWLEDGMENTS

The thanks of the author and the publishers are due to the following, for permission to quote extracts: George Allen and Unwin Ltd., *The Humanist Frame,* ed. Julian Huxley; Collins and Routledge and Kegan Paul, *Memories, Dreams, Reflections,* by C. G. Jung; Hodder and Stoughton Ltd., *G. A. Studdert Kennedy by his friends ("Sinner and Saint")*; the Society of Authors and Dr. John Masefield, O.M., *The Everlasting Mercy*; Mrs. George Bambridge and Messrs. Methuen and Macmillan Co. of Canada, *The King* and *The Explorer* by Rudyard Kipling; Oxford and Cambridge University Presses, *New English Bible, New Testament,* copyright 1961; the SCM Press Ltd. of London, *The Living of These Days* by Dr. H. E. Fosdick; A. D. Peters and Co., *Confessions of a Nihilist* by Eric Siepmann; Miss D. E. Collins, the owner of the late Mr. G. K. Chesterton's copyrights, and Messrs. Methuen and Co., Ltd., *The Song of the Strange Ascetic* by G. K. Chesterton.

Should an acknowledgment have been omitted inadvertently, then this oversight will be rectified in subsequent editions if brought to the attention of either the author or the publishers.

FOREWORD

WE live in a strange time. Agnostics are getting tired of their secularity just at the moment when many Christians seem to be getting tired of their certainties! It is spuriously recorded that when Gagarin came down from outer space Krushchev asked, secretly, whether he had seen any angels there. "I cannot tell a lie," said Gagarin, "I saw lots of angels there." Replied Krushchev, "I was afraid of that but do not tell the people, they are not ready for it yet." Lionised in Rome, Gagarin was sent for by the Pope. "Tell me," asked the Pope, "did you see any angels in the stratosphere?" "I cannot tell a lie," said Gagarin to His Holiness, "I did not see one angel there." "I was afraid of that," said the Pope, "but do not tell the people, they are not ready for it yet!" A strange time! The agnostics getting wistful, the believers losing certainty.

In such a day it is altogether good to be reminded that the main witness of the Church goes on true to the motto of Aberdeen University, "They say, what say they, let them say." Few ministers in Scotland have borne such a consistent witness through three decades as has Hugh Douglas to this consistent ministry. First buckling on his armour in the small town of Leven, then almost having to do battle with the conservatism that proverbially attends a down-town congregation in a changing day; now the acknowledged leader of all denominations in the Mother charge of Dundee.

A Chaplain to the Queen in Scotland, the skilled organiser of the great celebration of the fourth centenary of the Reformation in Scotland, he has a firm place in State and Church alike. But his real significance lies where all true ministry must reside—in his personal concern for people. His constant appearance on Scottish Television seals his reputation

7

as a "person-to-person" figure. His regular feature "Coping with Life" gives title to this book.

All the issues that assail the Church today are his province: bombs and bishops, sex and sleeping pills, gambling and gluttony. Just because he must constantly preach to ordinary folk, and keep it personal for the screen, and weekly attend marriage clinics, prison cells and Samaritan crises, he cannot dissociate any problem from its pressure on the man in the street.

For any who think the Church is on the defensive, or hard pressed (as countless newspaper articles would assume), this is a most salutary book.

"The kirk is an anvil that has worn out many hammers." Hugh Douglas gives ample proof that just as surely in 1964 as in 1564 the anvil still rings true. It is only those who persist in assuming that the Church is cracking who show themselves as "crackers".

GEORGE F. MacLEOD.

The Abbey,
Iona,
Argyll,
1964.

Note to the 1988 edition

The re-issue of *Coping with Life*, recalling the distinguished ministry of the late Dr Hugh Douglas, has been made possible by the support of

The Drummond Trust

CONTENTS

I

COPING WITH LIFE

AFTER a talk I once gave on television I received from a woman a letter in which she said, "The old nerves are as bad as ever. Why must life go on when there's no happiness in it? I have come to the conclusion that things work out for people in similar circumstances, but never in my case."

There is the cry of someone who feels unable to cope with life. It is typical of many others in this world of strange contrasts. Wealth is greater and more widely distributed, but two-thirds of humanity live in searing poverty. There is more material comfort, but more disharmony in personal relationships. In Britain we are exhorted to look forward to the rosy future of an expanding and affluent society, while a recent government survey tells us that we have become a nation of gamblers and debtors.

Medical science has practically abolished some diseases, but it has been unable to prevent a steep rise in others, particularly in nervous disorders. We have had over 1,900 years of the Christian religion, but there is a growing number of people who are conscious of what Sir Julian Huxley has called "a God-shaped blank" in their lives. Modern astronomy has shown us the immensity of the universe and the complete insignificance of this planet, let alone of ourselves as individuals. In consequence faith in the concern of a personal God in our affairs tends to wane, and a woman cries, "Why must life go on when there's no happiness in it?"

When people find themselves in such a predicament they may not completely reject the idea of some kind of divine power. The average person is reluctant to become a thorough-going atheist. He may retain a vague notion of God in the background of his mind, but consciously or unconsciously he looks for compensation in substitutes for Him. Thus one finds those who talk of fate, or luck, or destiny. They say, "Whatever will be will be," or, "If your name's on it you'll get it," or, "Wait for the lucky number." I sometimes wonder if the prevalence of this attitude is one of the reasons for the growth in the gambling habit and the remarkable popularity of the pools.

I have regularly received letters from various pools promoters, and I confess to having been touched by their personal interest in my welfare. Whether they think of me as having "a God-shaped blank" in my life or not, I cannot say, but they almost seem to regard themselves as father-substitutes in the concern which they show. "Dear friend," says one circular. O happy day! I am no longer a cog in a machine. I am singled out to be embraced in a close relationship. Somebody cares for me.

Even the reply-paid envelope enclosed for my use develops this theme. It bears a natty little badge. I observe the symbol of the clasped hands. Whose hands? How silly not to have twigged it sooner! This is myself and my pools promoter. It is written plain to see, "The Symbol of the Happy Circle." Now I know. We are all chums together. Should I still be in any doubt about my best interests being considered, I have only to turn to the reverse side of the circular. Beaming at me are the happy faces of all the other chums who have won anything from £200,000 to £300,000. Why should I not join their blissful band?

It may be, however, that I am the victim of doubts and a faithless scepticism. I still refrain from "investing" in the pools. (I like the word "investing". It builds up such a solid picture of sharing in whopping dividends). If so, the fatherly care is not diminished. I am sought out by further personal messages. One such came to me from a personable young woman (her photograph was on the letter), who again

addressed me as "Dear friend", and signed herself "Your
Pools Clerkess". The letter was couched in tender terms,
regretting that I had not begun to "invest", and indicating
that nothing would give her greater satisfaction than to hear
from me soon. Rudyard Kipling once wrote that "Romance
brought up the nine-fifteen". How sad that his pen should
have been confined to mundane subjects like railway trains,
and denied the opportunity of the rich glamour that lies
beneath the chequered surface of the weekly coupon!

The gambling habit continues to grow. I have heard a
psychiatrist describe it as an infantile regression. It has, on
the other hand, been justified as a harmless means of bringing
some excitement into lives which are drab and dull. I question the validity of such a thesis.

The fact that, in 1963, £1,000 million was spent in this
country on gambling of various kinds encourages me to
believe that the root cause is the simple desire to get something for nothing. Because people are unwilling to face up
to the adventure of living they seek a spurious satisfaction
in the gambling risk. Because they lack a vital and positive
belief in Providence the pools promoter (who is really the
only one to grow fat on the proceeds) cashes in on the need
for a universal provider. The pools would be no solution for
my depressed correspondent. She would always be sure that
someone else would hit the jack-pot of the treble chance.

Equally I doubt if she would find much comfort in reading
the astrology features in the daily press which appear under
such headings as "What the stars foretell". Few people,
perhaps, would confess to taking such features altogether
seriously. Yet the fact that they continue to appear indicates
the persistence of the superstition which accompanies a decay
in religious belief. I had often wondered how astrology came
to be taken up by the mass-circulation newspapers, but I had
found no clear explanation until I read the autobiography of
the late Arthur Christiansen, who was for many years editor
of the *Daily Express*.

Christiansen made it plain that the first astrology column appeared in the *Sunday Express* in 1930 as a publicity feature in the entertainment section of the paper. It was the year in which Princess Margaret was born, and it seemed a good idea to have her horoscope drawn up. Once begun, the feature continued. People took it seriously. If it said that Monday was a bad day for buying, claimed Christiansen, the buyers of more than one west-end store waited for the stars to become more propitious. Soon other papers followed suit, with the results which are familiar to us all. But what of the horoscope which began it all in 1930? Christiansen was curious enough to look it up thirty years later, and his only comment was, "How wrong you can be!"

It is interesting that those who find difficulty in believing that a personal God is concerned with them as individuals should take in any way seriously the notion that their lives are controlled by the movements of impersonal planets. If this is a substitute for religion, it is a poor one. It would scarcely soothe "the old nerves" which were as bad as ever. Anyone in such a plight would have to turn elsewhere.

Many seek refuge in anti-depressant drugs, sleeping pills and tranquillisers. It is no intention of mine merely to attack the use of these remedies or to deny that there are cases in which they are necessary. My concern is that they should not come to be regarded as providing the peace which passes understanding. I believe that the Christian Faith does this, and I am deeply sorry when I see those who think that religion has failed them turning to such substitutes. Rather than appear to be guilty of special pleading let me quote the objective evidence of an ITV edition of "This Week", shown in the autumn of 1963, as reported in *The Scotsman*.

According to the programme, half-a-million sleeping pills are sold every week and 1,500 people die every year, either by intentional or accidental overdoses. The death-roll has trebled in ten years and £2,000,000 is spent every year by the National Health Service on sleeping pills. It was also clear

from the evidence given by doctors appearing on the programme that it was often sheer lack of time which made
them prescribe pills which they knew would fail to solve their
patients' problems.

I was fairly sure that my correspondent would be getting
sleeping pills from her doctor, and I was more than certain
that if such was the case then "the old nerves" would continue
to plague her.

I could only tell her that I myself was no more immune
from worry than other people, and that I had known what it
was to lie awake at night and have the black depressing
thoughts circle round and round in unending succession. I
could also tell her that I had at least learned never to accept
any such thoughts as true, nor to make any decision in so
twisted a state of mind. I could assure her that I had known
what it was to make an act of trust in God and to find peace
breaking through. I could point her to the commandment
of Jesus which I had been compelled to accept, "Set your
mind on God's kingdom and His justice before everything
else, and all the rest will come to you as well. So do not be
anxious about tomorrow: tomorrow will look after itself.
Each day has troubles enough of its own."

She wrote later to say that things were rather better, but
I did not hear from her again. Such are the limitations of
long-range correspondence. By the same token, this is one
of the reasons for trying to write a book about coping with
life; and there are other letters which tell a more hopeful
story.

After another broadcast talk, letters came to me from two
widows who wrote quite independently of each other to say
how hard they found it to believe in God's care and purpose
for them. After having replied to them both, I heard no more
until two years later. Again they wrote quite independently
of each other, and again they wrote in similar terms. The
difference was that now they both said that they had, in their
own separate ways, discovered how remarkably life had worked

out for them, that it was still full of meaning and purpose, and that their hard experiences had in the end made them more sure of the Providence of God. They were coping with life.

This is a simple illustration, but it seems to me to be no less valid because of that. This is, after all, an uncomplicated book, written for ordinary people. In it I shall try to say something about my own experience of the Faith and of what others have taught me. Difficulties and failures have played their part both in teaching me lessons and in confirming my belief that there is no substitute for God.

I believe that men can find a far more satisfying outlet for their instinct for adventure than gambling. I remember having spent a Saturday afternoon with a compulsive gambler. We set off for a cinema and on the way we passed a dog-racing track. I could see that the man had to go through a severe inner struggle before he kept himself from going in. I saw him again years later. He was still a gambler, but of a different kind. He had decided, as it were, to bet his life there was a God, and he was working as a probation officer. His stakes were higher and his rewards were greater.

I believe that there is more to life than being the blind tool of impersonal forces. I believe that in all of us there is a spark of the divine, which reaches out for fulfilment. We can feel, in a deeper sense, the call which came to the explorer in Kipling's poem:

Something hidden. Go and find it. Go and look behind the
*   Ranges—*
Something lost behind the Ranges. Lost and waiting for you.
*   Go!*

I believe that life is not something which has to be made endurable by drugs. There is joy to be found in it. There is creative activity which lies within the grasp of anyone who has discovered the clue to living in Jesus Christ. *Coping with*

Life is not meant to be a negative title. It does not imply resignation. Rather does it seek to point to renewal.

I cannot claim to offer any nicely-packaged prescription for victorious living. I simply believe that it is a reality which can be experienced. In the pages which follow I shall try to set down some of the reasons which have made me more certain that this is so.

2

ENCOUNTER WITH GOD

WHAT makes one become a Christian? Heredity and environment? It means a great deal to be born into a Christian family, baptised in the Christian Church and brought up in the atmosphere of Christianity. On the face of it, the secular analysis of human nature as being conditioned by heredity and environment might seem to apply equally to Christians. But it does not in fact do so. There is a third (and often forgotten) factor. There is God.

Think of St. Paul. Three cities played important parts in his life. They were Tarsus, Jerusalem and Damascus. Tarsus stood for his environment. It was the city in which he was brought up, a great trading centre. There he was born a Roman citizen. In it he absorbed the influence of Greek culture. Jerusalem, on the other hand, represented his heredity. He was a Hebrew of the Hebrews, and he went there to train as a rabbi, studying under Gamaliel. To this extent he was conditioned by heredity and environment; and because of them he was a bitter opponent of the early Christian Church.

But on the road to Damascus, God came into his life in a new and overpowering way. "Christ took hold of me," he said later. Damascus was decisive in his life. Now the frustrating tensions were resolved. All that Tarsus and Jerusalem had given him could be used for his own fulfilment and for the work of spreading the Faith through Asia Minor, Greece and Rome. His heredity and his environment were preparations for the purpose which God had planned all along.

We may think that we make up our minds about God. It is even as if we decided to summon Him into existence by our decisions. But it is God who has made His mind up about *us*. He always makes the first move, and our decisions, when they are made, are in response to His seeking of us.

When I think of the stages in my life which led me to membership of the Church and then to the ministry, I see how much I owe to other people. I had to learn about Christianity from them. We all have to do this. It is through other people that God can speak to us. His purpose works out in what seem to be very ordinary ways. There may be no voices from heaven, no mystical experience, no ecstatic visions. Yet all the time God can be at work with us, even when we do not realise it.

For myself, I owe a very great debt to my parents. I think I realised this more clearly when my wife and I sailed into Bombay harbour in 1962 on our way home from Australia. I had not been in Bombay since 1919, when, as a child of seven, I had seen the gap widening between the ship and the quay as I left my parents on my way home to Scotland. As we berthed now at the same spot, I remembered vividly the sick feeling of desolation I had had when I realised that it would be years before I should see them again. I resented the separation. It made it hard to pick up the threads of the relationship when we met again. I suppose I might easily have blamed Christianity for this experience, been more diffi-cult and rebellious than I was, and ended up as a thorough-going agnostic. But things worked out differently.

I always feel that I missed a lot by having been separated from my father, except when he came home on furlough every five years. My mother stayed at home for one five-year period, which was another sacrifice for him, but a great benefit to me. In one sense I lacked the normal steady home life of a united family, but my parents were wise and patient in their dealing with me. I can see more and more how much their example counted. This was brought home to me again in 1962, when we visited the mission station at Jalna on the Deccan plateau, where my father had gone as a young missionary in 1894. We received a tremendous welcome, and it was simply because my parents were still remembered there. One old *bai* clasped my hands in her own, with tears in her eyes, and poured out a flood of Marathi. She was telling me that as a famine orphan she had been sold in the bazaar for a rupee, probably to be brought up as a prostitute. But the mission had rescued her. My father had baptised her, and years later he had taken her wedding service. She wanted to thank me for what he had done.

Later, on that same day, I found one of the hospital staff waiting to see me in the bungalow. Once more he had a story to tell of how much he owed to my father. "Hugh *baba*," he said, "I remember the advice he gave me when I was a young boy. He told me to be content with the simple life, to be completely honest in everything, and always to be loyal to my Master, Jesus Christ. I want you to know how much it has meant to me all my life."

Although I had not heard this story before, I could well imagine my father having said that. This was his own way of life. He was a man of great integrity. Like other missionaries, he and my mother never had much money, but I never once heard them complain or show resentment. They were very hospitable and generous, much more willing to give than to receive, and with them both "cheerfulness was always breaking in". Again, like other missionaries, they had to sacrifice a good deal. Their first child, my elder brother, died of cholera in Jalna and his grave is in the cemetery there. I know my mother could never forget that heartbreak, but she was never bitter about it. She and my father lived out their Christianity with direct simplicity. This made an impression upon me which was decisive.

It surprises me, therefore, when I hear materialists saying that men create their own moral values and that our behaviour is the product of the society in which we live. My parents were representative of many other Christian people who took the way of self-denial around the turn of the nineteenth century. This was the golden age of the British Empire, a time of unparalleled wealth, ease and luxury, at least among the upper classes. Sir Osbert Sitwell has told us how his grandfather, the Earl of Londesborough, enjoyed an annual income of £100,000, and that when he and his family chose to have a walk at Scarborough, a mile of red carpet was laid from their house to the promenade.

Such were the pressures of society and the values which were rated highest by many people. In spite of this there would seem to have been many others, like my parents, who were not impressed or conditioned by such values. In contrast, they took quite literally the call to deny themselves and take up their cross and follow Christ. I would say that it was they who were right and society which was wrong. They acted as they did because of their belief in Jesus Christ as the way, the truth, and the life. His values were not created by the society in which He lived. When He was crucified it was the society of His time which put Him to death. The title on His cross, written in Greek, Latin and Hebrew, was a symbol of His rejection by the Greek, Roman and Hebrew civilizations.

The example of Christian parents, then, is of the first importance in the making of a Christian. Along with that should go a real contact with the worship and life of the Church. From their earliest years, children should be accustomed to thinking of church as the place where they go with their parents, as a family.

I once had a discussion on TV with a pleasant young journalist who was an agnostic. As we were talking afterwards he told me that he intended to send his children to the local Sunday school, although he did not attend church himself. I realised that he had good intentions, but I tried to point out that there was little value in the idea. Apart from the question of the quality of the teaching in the Sunday school, the Christian Faith is not just something to be taught like an

academic subject, least of all to young children. It is a way
of life, an attitude of the whole personality, which has to be
communicated in the wholeness of living rather than "taught"
in a semi-intellectual fashion. That young man wanted to
have his cake and eat it. I suggested that he would have to
come off the fence before the iron entered his soul, and that
the only real way of showing his children the meaning of
Christianity was by taking them with him to church, not
by sending them to Sunday school while he stayed at home
and read the Sunday newspapers.

To be truthful, I myself rebelled in the normal way against
going to church with my parents. I found it a dull and un-
interesting way of passing the time. The sermons were apt
to last for forty-five minutes and the prayers were correspond-
ingly long. My mind inevitably wandered, and I used to go
in detail through the rugger matches I had played in or
watched the previous day.

On the whole I preferred the services in the little country
church at the fishing village in Kintyre where we spent our
holidays. They were less formal. One knew that there would
be a bathe or a picnic in the afternoon. Other families, with
whom one shared in the fun of the holiday, were there. In
fact, even for a youngster, the fellowship and the link between
life and worship were more obvious. But although in the
city I had to endure the remoteness and formality of church
worship—as it seemed to me then—I knew that it meant
something of supreme importance to my parents. What, to
begin with, was a habit imposed upon me by precept and
example became in time a vital and essential part of my own
experience.

I am sure that we must recapture—and here I speak of the
Christian community—the practice of the family going to
church together. Here the responsibility lies squarely upon
the shoulders of Christian parents. They take every possible
precaution for the health of their children—vaccinations, in-
jections, dental treatments, and all the rest. They are most

anxious that they should get into the right kind of school and pass the necessary examinations. They put themselves to no end of trouble to give them the best possible start in life, and yet they can be appallingly careless or slack about the supremely important factor, which is that of showing them that in their daily lives they need the help and guidance of God.

Children do not know this any more than they know that they ought to brush their teeth regularly or wash their hands before eating. They have to be shown and trained in these habits. It is the same with Christian upbringing. There is not the slightest danger in discipline when it is the discipline of love. I like the story which Dr. H. E. Fosdick tells of his own boyhood. His father was leaving the house one morning and called to his wife, "Tell Harry he can cut the grass today, if he feels like it." Then he turned back at the door and added, "Tell Harry he had better feel like it!" A good example of parental responsibility.

There is also a responsibility laid upon the Church to make its services more meaningful and relevant, particularly to young people. I am writing these words on the island of Iona, where every summer hundreds of young people come to the youth camps run by the Iona Community. In the Abbey services they find worship coming alive for them. It is an expression of the fellowship, the fun and the gaiety they have together. It reflects the beauty of the island, the wonderful colours of sea and rock, in the reality of its devotional language and in the strong gladness of its praise. It challenges them to be concerned about the problems they face in the cities from which they come, the rat-race and the materialistic pressures in modern society, the issue of peace and war, the needs of the hungry and under-privileged peoples of the world. I know from experience how many lads and girls have been given, through worship like this, a new vision of the meaning of life. This is what the Church should be seeking to do, more and more.

In my own youth there was no Iona Community, but a comparable influence in my religious development was the Scottish Schoolboys' Club, with its linked activity, the Glasgow Sunday Meetings. The S.S.C. ran Easter camps for schoolboys from the east and west of Scotland. The G.S.M. had meetings on Sunday nights in private houses. The leaders were Christians (always Church members) who had a gift for working with boys—men like Stanley Nairne, Duggie Smith and Willie Boyd—and of communicating a simple, straightforward and manly version of the Gospel. Several international rugger players among the leaders gave an additional incentive for hero-worshipping youngsters to come along.

The appeal of the S.S.C. was primarily the real fellowship which it expressed. Easter camps were tremendous fun. After a day of games and outdoor activities there was a sing-song which was as riotous as it was hilarious. The transition to a short evening service was completely natural; and in the quietness of the huge marquee in which it was held, the simple words of the speaker—unpretentious and sincere—gave a deep impression of the reality of God and the challenge and appeal of Jesus Christ. I am glad to see that in this more sophisticated era the S.S.C. is still carrying on the good work which helped me so much all those years ago.

Another potent influence in the communication of religion can be the school. Unfortunately it is not always so. In Scotland, at least, religion is not at the moment an examinable subject in the school curriculum, and there is a gentleman's agreement in Education Authority Schools (with the exception of Roman Catholic schools) by which religious instruction is given to senior pupils in two periods during the week. The quality of this instruction depends upon the interest shown by the headmaster in the subject as a whole, and upon the belief and ability of the individual teacher who gives the instruction. There is thus an obviously variable element in the situation which prevents one from making any dogmatic statement. But it is fair to say that there is a general feeling in Church circles that if there is cause for dissatisfaction with the Church's own system of religious education, this dissatisfaction also extends to the religious instruction which is given in schools.

In the school I attended—Glasgow Academy—there was hardly any religious instruction at all. Our official religion was Christianity, but our real religion (as a school) was Rugby football. Our academic activity was kept in its proper place, as a necessary evil sandwiched between the ritual attendances on Saturdays at New Anniesland, where the Glasgow Academicals were at the height of their fame. They had a beautifully drilled team which included a complete back division of Scottish internationalists.

One of their most loyal supporters was Dr. James Moffatt, famous for his translation of the New Testament and himself an Academical. It is told that he was asked to open a sale of work on the Saturday when the Academicals were due to play their great rivals, Heriot's, at Anniesland. Torn between desire and duty, he nevertheless opened the sale of work.

The following Monday one good lady was describing the occasion to a neighbour. "How fortunate we were," she said, "to have Dr. Moffatt with us. But he is such a busy man! He had to hurry away to be at an open-air meeting at Anniesland."

Glasgow Academy was—as it still is—a good school. We were certainly not made to work ourselves into nervous wrecks, but the academic record was good. Our religious observances were not such as to arouse resentment against forcible indoctrination; but the Academy has produced a good proportion of ministers and Christian laymen.

Morning prayers were held daily, in the old gymnasium, for the upper school, who stood in restless ranks with a prefect behind each group. The Rector, Edwin Temple, conducted prayers from a rough rostrum, and we gabbled responsively through the Psalms without much idea of what the language meant. Any signs of inattention or irreverence were corrected by the prefects, by the unorthodox but effective method of kicking the offender hard in the seat of his pants.

How much of the beauty of holiness this instilled into us I cannot say. But of this I am certain: no Academy boy of my time left the school without having come to know that "Ted", our Rector, was a believing and practising Christian. He had a tremendous influence for good, which made up for any deficiencies in the methods of religious instruction which were then employed. This is not to justify inadequacy in this field, but is mentioned simply as an example of the power for good which an individual can exercise.

Home, Church and school can play their part in laying the foundations of belief. There still remains the decisive encounter with God for each individual, the response to God's activity, which (for the Christian) is shown in his baptism. Martin Luther, in moments of depression, used to write down the words, *"Baptizatus sum"*—"I have been baptized"—to recall himself to the battle of faith.

When I left school and went to Glasgow University there was no thought in my mind of such an experience as this. Nominally I was a Christian, having become a communicant member of the Church mainly because my parents wished me to, before they returned to India from furlough. I had not found this an exciting or moving experience. I had received only two short and quite inadequate periods of instruction, and was "admitted to participation in the Lord's Supper" (the word "Confirmation" was not normally used then in the Church of Scotland) at a thinly attended pre-Communion Service at which I was the solitary first communicant. At this stage I intended to become a lawyer, and read some law subjects along with my classical course.

Being on my own, with my parents in India, was a useful experience. It was confusing and exhilarating to be pitchforked into a bustling cosmopolitan university to rub shoulders with all sorts of people. I lived in one of the residential Halls, and soon discovered that the Christian Faith could no longer be taken for granted.

I remember several likeable students who argued persuasively on behalf of Bertrand Russell's rejection of Christianity, and urged me to read his little book, *Why I am not a Christian*. I did so, and found his arguments uncomfortably telling and forceful, especially when I had scant philosophical or apologetic equipment to deal with them. But at the back of my mind there was the persistent thought that Russell and Christ could not both be right. I would have to choose between them. I had my doubts and I knew something of what it was to flirt with the agnostic position, but I was also prepared to doubt my doubts.

Again I should say that I found God through other people. It was comparatively easy to see the difference in the university community between Christians and non-Christians. One met so many different types. There were some attractive characters who had decided that university life suited them admirably, who stayed on year after year, and who got regularly, if courteously, sozzled every Saturday night. There were the types who "lived it up" with women and scoffed at Christian moral standards. It did not seem to me that they had found the secret of full and happy living.

There was a real danger of becoming something of a prig in such a situation, and I am glad that various activities kept me from spending too much time in religious circles. It was thus possible to take a more objective view, and while I must say that I found some of the non-Christians most friendly, interesting and amusing, there was never any real doubt in my mind that the Christians had something which the others lacked.

I was also helped, on the intellectual level, by the influence of men like Archie Craig, the University Chaplain, and A. A. Bowman, who was then Professor of Moral Philosophy. I remember particularly a meeting in the University Union which was addressed by Dean Inge. Unfortunately he was not at his best and gave a disappointing talk. This was about the time when he had been described as being less a pillar of the Church than two columns in the *Evening Standard*. And I could see, from my seat in the gallery, that he was in fact reading, in a desultory fashion, from a collection of newspaper cuttings. The meeting was saved from anti-climax only when A. A. Bowman rose to move a vote of thanks. Sensing the atmosphere, he spoke with burning conviction for forty-five minutes on Tertullian's saying about Christianity, "I believe it because it is unbelievable, I believe it because it is absurd". Hearing him, I felt that Bertrand Russell had little to offer in comparison.

All this time I was moving, although scarcely aware of it, towards a decisive encounter. As is often the case, this came about in a normal and apparently insignificant way. I had to prepare an outline for a course of talks which was to be given at a boys' camp. One of them was about "Vocation", and I was forced to ask myself what my vocation in life was going to be. I had more or less drifted into reading for law, but was it going to be my calling? Or could it be that I should change over and prepare for the ministry?

I resisted the idea. I felt that I was not sure enough in my belief. Being a solitary type, I talked to no one about this, and as letters to India took three weeks to arrive, I did not ask my parents' advice. It was quite an intense and lonely struggle. I heard no divine voice speaking clearly, and there seemed to be no direct answer through prayer. Once again a human voice spoke. I had dropped in to an evening service in a local church. Few people were there and everything was normal and outwardly rather dull. But something which the preacher said, and the sincerity with which he communicated his own belief in God, spoke decisively to me. I decided that my vocation was to be a minister.

There had been nothing dramatic or outstanding in my spiritual pilgrimage so far. I have outlined it simply because it shows, I believe, the average human influences and pressures which can affect ordinary people.

There are many others who will have more exciting tales of rebellion and conversion to tell. I am sure they are authentic. My claim, however, is that God can show Himself just as surely and as clearly to individuals in plain and simple ways. He is always seeking them. He is to be found in the events of their daily lives, and above all in their meeting and relationships with other people. When we think of the slender and tenuous threads which have led us to moments which have changed the whole course of our lives, we can see that nothing is too insignificant for God to use. What we ourselves need is an awareness which makes us willing to look for His action, so that when the time comes we may be ready to respond.

There is no limit to the ways in which God can speak to the human heart. Some people are drawn to Him through the strong fellowship of a group or church. Others see the example of an individual whom they admire, and say to themselves, "If a person like that can believe in God, there must be something in such belief." Many, especially in modern times, become Christians because they have found life impossible and see in the Faith a new and hopeful path.

I have known those who made their decisions at crowded evangelistic meetings, and those who have come to God in the loneliness of their own rooms. I have met others to whom God spoke through a radio or TV broadcast or in a normal church service. There are some who have grown so naturally in Christian experience that they could scarcely point to a time when they did not believe. Others again, like Francis Thompson the poet, have tried to run away and have found it impossible to escape the Hound of Heaven.

I remember talking with such a man. He was left-wing and rebellious, agin' the Government, the Establishment and the Kirk. Looking at him I could see his innate goodness. "Bert," I said, "the Hound of Heaven will catch up with you one day." So indeed He did, and I have known no more sincere or faithful Christian than this one-time rebel.

God may speak differently to us all and we may come to Him in an infinite variety of ways, but for all of us there must be some decisive encounter where we see that we have to choose. This is a moment of truth. It is the real beginning of the response of faith to God's seeking of us. As the Letter to the Hebrews says, "Anyone who comes to God must believe that He exists and that He rewards those who search for Him."

3

CHALLENGE TO YOUTH

LOOKING back on my own experience I am bound to ask myself if the claims of Christianity are less likely to make an impact upon modern youth. Certainly the materialistic pressures upon them are much stronger and more persuasive than they were between the two world wars. At that time there was no TV, and sound broadcasting was not long past its infancy. The "talkies" had only just begun, and little was said about the influence of mass media. Even our reading was unsophisticated in comparison with today.

Leaving aside *Lady Chatterley's Lover*, think only of the contrast between two fictional heroes of best-selling thrillers, John Buchan's Richard Hannay, and Ian Fleming's James Bond. Hannay was a perfect example of the clean-cut, good-living English sportsman. He never stooped to foul play. Having married the heroine of his earlier exploits, he remained faithful to her and lived happily with his family in the intervals between his adventures.

Bond, on the other hand, is an amoral and unprincipled bachelor. Often engaged in desperate struggles with the Russian Secret Service, he outmatches their shadiest tricks. No Bond story is complete without his having violently killed several opponents (he is, of course a deadly shot and an expert at in-fighting), suffered various sadistic tortures and slept with a variety of glamorous and accommodating young women. One does not take thrillers too seriously, but the difference in the climates of opinion represented by Hannay and Bond is significant.

There is considerable concern about the moral condition

of our country today, and it would be easy to take the line of denouncing contemporary decadence. We are only too familiar with the statistics of crime and juvenile delinquency, of pre-nuptial conceptions and illegitimate births, of divorce and broken homes. There is a morbid pre-occupation with "sex", shown in many plays, films, books and newspapers, and spreading over into the field of advertising.

The Profumo and Ward affairs, with their evidence of the habits of the characters involved, threw a more lurid light upon a situation which was well known to exist, but which had not previously been brought so blatantly to public notice. It is not, however, my intention merely to denounce. It is the notorious affairs which get the headlines in the news. Little or nothing is said about the great number of people who still do their best to hold to the Christian standards in their homes and families and in their public lives.

What does concern me more is the cynical and sophisticated approach which seeks to justify (on a pseudo-intellectual basis) the general laxity in morals which we see today. Even some of our Christian apologists seem to be influenced by these trends of thought, and give the impression (however excellent may be their intentions) that the Christian moral standards will have to be relaxed. Such are the pressures which make it more difficult for young people to see the Christian way clearly.

One of our greatest troubles is that for so many in our country possessions seem to matter more than people. I personally found it far more shocking to read about Rachman's slum empire than any of the other sordid details of the case which brought his activities to light. Here was the deliberate and cold-blooded exploitation of human beings who needed homes to live in, and who were given appalling hovels at exorbitant rents, and who, if they dared to protest, were harried and beaten up by hired thugs.

It has always seemed to me that Christian indignation and denunciation should primarily be directed against activities of this kind. Ever since I worked as a young man and then as a minister in the slums of Glasgow (than which there are no worse in Europe), I have had a burden on my conscience about the conditions in which so many of our fellow-citizens have had to exist. These slums were first built because men were more concerned with possessions than with people; and at the height of Victorian evangelicalism there were too few Christians like Octavia Hill who sought to remedy the conditions, let alone protest against them.

That slums still exist, in spite of all the programmes of re-housing, is a continuing challenge to the Christian con-science—and also to young people who seek an outlet for their idealism. It is encouraging to hear of individuals and groups who are concerned enough to live among and identify themselves with those who are "socially undesirable".

This is being done by the East Harlem Protestant Church in New York and by the Gorbals Group in Glasgow.

These experiments are based on the same principle. This is that to most of the people who live in the East Harlem or Gorbals slums the organised Church seems infinitely remote and apparently unconcerned. Thus those who are members of both groups live in the areas where they are working. They share to some extent the conditions of their neighbours. They run clubs and do family case-work in the normal way, but with a more immediate sense of neighbourliness than would otherwise be possible. They concern themselves with cases of exploitation by landlords where, for example, thirty to forty people live in a seven-roomed flat in complete squalor and at exorbitant rents. They know that they have taken on a tough job, but they find it worth doing.

Such experiments may be small in number and limited to the few idealists who are prepared to undertake them, but they are challenging and significant. They give practical expression to a concern which should be felt much more deeply than it is by the Christian community as a whole.

If possessions continue to matter more than people in the

public mind, the provision of better housing will not in itself solve our deep-rooted problems. I remember finding myself in a railway carriage with a lad being taken by an escort to a Borstal institution, after he had run away for the third time from an approved school. I had a lot to do with Jock after that, without making much impression upon him. He was caught and held by the results of possessions mattering more than people. His parents had more or less given him up as a bad job, and they were mainly concerned with earning enough themselves to meet their needs.

On his release from Borstal he went straight, for the year of his licence, but he was not making enough money as an apprentice to satisfy him. He took what he thought was the easy way of "doing a job" with some others, was caught, and received his first prison sentence. He wrote to me from there:

"I am keeping fine, hoping you are the same. I had a letter from my mother. She says I am not getting back to the house. I have only myself to blame for that, so when I come out of prison I will have at least one problem to keep me company. I know I have been a headache for you ever since we first met, but that is just the way things were meant to be."

Here was a good home in a new housing scheme. There was nothing wrong with the material conditions, but the personal relationships had gone wrong. His parents had lost all patience as well as any friendly contact with him. What mattered most to him—on the surface at least—was easy money; and he allowed himself to be a fatalistic escapist—"that is just the way things were meant to be." But the way things were meant to be for him, as for everyone, was that he should have seen that other people mattered because he himself mattered to God.

Where men lose an awareness of God there is a spiritual vacuum left in their lives which nothing material can fill. When I visited Sweden in 1961 I was impressed by the excellence of material conditions. There were no slums, no unemployment, complete social security with first-rate health insurance and hospital services, and liberal retirement pensions.

But the Churchmen I talked with were concerned about the state of the Church as well as of the country. Over ninety per cent of the Swedish people were nominally members of the National Church, but active membership was limited to a small proportion. In spite of all the material advantages there was a very high rate of divorce, illegitimacy, alcoholism, suicide and nervous breakdowns. There was a large number of young people in nerve hospitals. I had an uncomfortable feeling that this was where our own Welfare State was heading if we continued to concentrate on possessions rather than people. Where there is a spiritual vacuum individuals try to fill it with substitutes like alcohol and sex-adventures; and when these inevitably fail they seek an escape through drugs or suicide. A man's life does *not* consist of the abundance of his possessions.

If Christians know this to be true they must get their message across in a positive way. I remember a big open-air meeting arranged by a group of ministers. There was a platform for the speakers, with loudspeaker equipment. There had been good publicity and a large crowd had gathered to hear what the Church had to say. But they heard nothing at first, because the loudspeakers did not function. One of the ministers began working with the equipment, and suddenly his voice boomed out across the crowd: "That's what was wrong! The positive was in the negative!" The wires had been crossed; the positive lead was in the negative socket.

This was a parable of how, when the Church gives the impression of continually condemning, its real message is lost. If, indeed, people matter more than possessions, we have to show positively, both by word and action, that this is so. There is a fruitful field for this in every Christian congregation. In Stewardship activity a new outlet of concern and service can be found, and from within the congregation this can spread out into the community.

This indeed is happening all over the world, and wherever there has been an effective Stewardship campaign there has been a new upsurge of life as men and women have felt again the power of the Spirit. For Stewardship is far more than a means of raising more money. It is a way in which we can offer to God, in service of Him and of others, all that we have and are. I saw this working in Australia, and I have seen it in this country. It is authentic and positive. It gives meaning and purpose to our membership in the Church.

Meaning and purpose are what young people are looking for today. Often they fail to find them in contemporary society. Indeed the magnitude of world problems conjoined with their own lack of any sure basis for living can produce in them a sense of frustrated cynicism. They may be well endowed with brains and well equipped by academic or business training, but none the less they "lose the place", and drift aimlessly. They may seek the answer on a psychiatrist's couch and still fail to find it. Of one such his father wrote to me that what his son needed most was some deep and simple wisdom to show him the way out of the sophistries in which he was entangled.

This, I am sure, is a typical case. Because the Christian Faith seems too simple in a scientific age, it can be scorned by those who take a certain pride in their intellectual ability. They do not realise how deep it goes, how demanding and challenging its apparent simplicity can be, how true it is when it is tested and tried in the experience of life.

Jesus was right when he said that the truths of the Kingdom were hidden from the wise and the prudent and revealed unto babes. Eric Siepmann, in his book *Confessions of a Nihilist*, in which he describes his rebellion against and his return to Christianity, asks the following question of himself, "So it took you a life-time of experiments, errors and revolt to discover something you were told in your nursery, and which every simple, uncomplicated person knows from birth?"

To which he gives the answer "Yes!"

One sees the point of this. The most subtle and complicated philosophical arguments are really dealing with the same questions which a simple old woman sitting in a garret has already answered intuitively through her belief in God. The philosopher seeks to make explicit in theory what has already been found to be true in their experience by countless humble believers. This is not to deny that intellectuals and philosophers are necessary, but it is to say that they have no prescriptive right to the last word about the meaning and purpose of human life.

It is for this reason that I would take up the cudgels with the contemporary attack upon Christian moral standards. I have noticed for some time the tendency to ridicule as Puritans those who stand for chastity before marriage and fidelity after marriage. The implication is that they represent a narrow and restricted approach to life. They miss, it is said, the freedom and joy of unshackled living. I wonder.

As a parish minister I see this question at both ends, so to speak. I know the tensions and struggles through which young people can pass. I have heard them arguing that surely there can be nothing wrong in sleeping with someone of whom you are fond and whom you intend to marry. I have listened to their plea that with earlier physical maturity and long courses of professional training it is an undue strain to postpone the physical relationship until marriage is economically possible. And I still hold to what is called the Puritan view. One reason is that I have seen too many instances of those who have thrown over the traces and who have not only lost their integrity, but have also found the reverse of happiness as a result.

My main reason, however, is that I believe that the teaching of Jesus is quite plain and uncompromising on this issue. There has been considerable misunderstanding of the biblical teaching on the man-woman relationship, for which the Church itself has been partly to blame. From the time of the

Desert Fathers onwards the impression has been given that Christians look on this relationship, on the physical side, with a sense of shame and guilt. But this is not the biblical view. There is, in fact, a strong if slender thread running through the Bible from Genesis to the Epistles. To summarise it most briefly, it maintains that the relationship is God-given and good, designed to find its fulfilment in the lasting union of marriage.

I cannot agree with the attempt to cast the mantle of Christianity over unchastity before marriage. There is not the slightest justification for this in the teaching of Jesus. It is true that He condemned the sins of the spirit more strongly than the sins of the flesh, but He did not condone fornication. It is an entirely false antithesis to imply, as Professor G. M. Carstairs did in his third Reith lecture, that charity is more important than chastity. They are not alternatives or mutually exclusive. They are both Christian virtues, and as such they each have to be practised by Christians. This is a free country, and people are entitled to proclaim the merits of lack of chastity if they so desire; but they are not entitled on any count to claim that to be unchaste is to be Christian, any more than they are entitled to imply that sinners will not be treated with charity by Christians.

If there is a misunderstanding of biblical teaching there is also, to my mind, a false view abroad of what "sex" means. In the popular representation given to it "sex" would appear to mean the physical relationship by itself. Thus one of the girls who gave evidence in the Ward trial spoke of going into the bedroom of the flat and "having sex" with a man. One can only say that this is a pitiful and inadequate caricature of what sex should be. It is not limited to brief animal encounters, whether they are bought by money or not. It should be a total relationship of persons, involving the whole personality, an expression of their love for each other and a union of body, mind and spirit. Wherever it falls short of this it inevitably brings frustration instead of fulfilment.

Thus I oppose the current advocacy of moral laxity on two grounds. The first is that I reject the theory of relative standards. As a Christian I have to accept the teaching of Jesus as having an absolute claim on my loyalty. I may indeed come far short, in many respects, of living up to that teaching, but I must retain my belief in its authority.

The second ground of my opposition is empirical, based on my own experience and that of other people. I know that there is happiness and fulfilment in keeping to the standards of chastity and fidelity. If this is Puritanism then I am glad to be a Puritan, and to have many others as my friends whom I know as gay, happy and interesting people who find life fascinating and fulfilling. I cannot say that I have found the same to be true of those who flit from one sex adventure to another or who have to endure the tensions of broken personal relationships. I meet many such in, for example, marriage guidance counselling, and the poor souls are invariably in a sad state of confusion and depression.

I think that it is a pity that men of the character, background and calibre of Professor Carstairs should give the impression that they support the humanist rather than the straightforward Christian view. In his third Reith lecture he referred to Paul's influence on the Christian attitude to sex, and called him "an intemperate disciple, an authoritarian character, who introduced the concept of celibacy as an essential part of Christian teaching". This is a shallow and inadequate analysis. It fails to take account of the situation which existed in Corinth when Paul wrote to the Corinthians about moral behaviour, or of the fact that he was writing in the belief that the world was shortly to come to an end.

Corinth in Paul's time was a thriving commercial city which had the reputation of being the richest, the most beautiful and the wickedest place in Greece. The heights of Acro-Corinth were dominated by the temple of Aphrodite (or Venus), the goddess of physical love. In the temple were

1,000 prostitutes whose religious duty it was to ply their trade in the city. This was what "sex" meant in Corinth.

What Paul did—and I wonder if Professor Carstairs has tried to see this—was to introduce a radically new idea of the relationship between man and woman, based on his own understanding of the Christian Faith. In contrast with the sultry and sordid activities of the temple of Aphrodite he spoke of the body as being the temple of the Holy Spirit. In place of the frustration of inadequate personal relationships he called for the purity and simplicity of Christian homes. Over against the limited notion of love as being Eros (physical passion) he set the challenge of love as Agape in the glorious hymn of 1 Corinthians 13. He realised the need for the physical expression of love (1 Corinthians 7: 1–7) even although he was sure of the imminent end of the world. He was stern in his denunciation of a case of incest (1 Corinthians 5: 1) and later he was urging full compassion and forgiveness for the offender (2 Corinthians 2: 5–11). In the context of the situation with which he was dealing I fail to see how he can fairly be described as intemperate or authoritarian, or as having laid it down for all time that celibacy should be an essential part of Christian teaching. He was at pains to draw a distinction between the advice he gave in a local situation and the unchanging teaching of Jesus. His overpowering concern was to bring the Christians at Corinth out of darkness into God's marvellous light.

And indeed the situation both in Greece and in Rome was one of darkness and messy moral decadence. It surprises me when I hear the advocates of pre-marital intercourse speaking of it (as Professor Carstairs has done) as "a sensible preliminary to marriage" and as "a rewarding experience". Nor am I impressed when Dr. Comfort, in a TV discussion, informs us that it is a good thing for a man to have two women. (I should, incidentally, like to hear what the two women had to say about it.)

These are no new ideas. They were practised with consider-

able zeal in the ancient world and were merely symptoms of
the decay into which it was sinking. Even the pagan thinkers
and writers were disgusted by the behaviour of their contemporaries, as is shown by the Roman poet Juvenal in his
sixth Satire. In fact the modern idealization of sexual experi-
mentation would strike me as being both antiquated and
ludicrous if it did not have deep undertones of tragedy.

Typical of the modern scene as portrayed by writers was
one of those vast American novels which I tried to read. I
gave it up after (I think) page 37, where the hero was recorded
as having his first extra-marital and presumably rewarding
experience on a library sofa. (At least it was not a public
library, but perhaps this stage of emancipation from Puritan
restraints remains as a height to be scaled.)

If this is life, liberty and the pursuit of happiness, give me
Paul every time and call me a reactionary by all means. He
was fighting for what he believed to be the truth of God. He
knew the misery and degradation of the human situation
with which he was dealing, which was not unlike our own.
He sought to release people from the chains of self into
the liberty of the children of God, to lift them from the
frustrations of mere passion into the fulfilment of love.
In fact, he did this; and it ill becomes, for example, Dr.
Eustace Chesser to point to him as "one of the world's
most influential and therefore perhaps most dangerous sex
reactionaries".

I am glad that I know many young people who are sufficiently independent and clear-thinking not to be taken in by
slick refurbishing of old and mistaken ideas. But I would
suggest that there is a heavy burden of responsibility upon
those who criticise the Christian standards and call for their
relaxation.

Tourists today can still see the wall-paintings at Pompeii.
Many of them are far from edifying and represent the love-
life of Jupiter, king of the gods of ancient Rome. That great
classical scholar and Christian, T. R. Glover, wrote of how

the Latin dramatist, Terence, pictured a young man looking at these paintings and saying to himself, "If Jupiter did it, why should not I?" Similarly today there can be young people who, without understanding much of what is involved, will say "If so-and-so says that it is O.K., why shouldn't I do it?" Let them remember that the world began in any real sense to think of people as persons rather than things only after Jesus had come. If, indeed, personal relationships are the very heart and centre of living, we must learn from Him what it means to love God and to love our neighbours as ourselves. He is the supreme authority and His standards do not change, because they are of God.

When I was a student at Glasgow University the Senate decided to confer a honorary degree on the great violinist Fritz Kreisler. Glasgow graduations in those days could be riotous and unruly occasions, but this one was different. For half-an-hour a mob of undergraduates remained in spellbound silence as Kreisler played to them most wonderfully on his violin. He was entirely free to do what he chose with his instrument, with supreme artistry. But his freedom depended upon the rigorous discipline to which he had first subjected himself. He was the master of his art because he had first surrendered himself to becoming its servant. This was true freedom, and it was as different as could be from the licence of an untutored child drawing its bow across the violin strings in a series of jangled discords.

Any art, skill or profession demands discipline before the freedom of mastery can be achieved; and the thrill of the mastery is to enjoy the achievement to the full—within the prescribed and inevitable limits. No game can be played or enjoyed without its rules and the boundaries for the field of play. In the intricate, complex and demanding sphere of our relationships with each other we cannot reverse the process and follow our unregulated desires. If we want harmony in our living we must first be in harmony with God. "Love God and do what you like," said St. Augustine. This is true, but only if we first have accepted the discipline of Jesus, Who is the supreme Master in the art of living.

I hold no brief for the Puritans of the seventeenth century. I do not think that they had the answer, but I am sure that Jesus has it. In the tensions of today there is a need for those who have the courage and the sense to be Positive Puritans. Robert Burns, who knew as much as anyone about unbridled licence, also knew what he had missed when he made his Muse address him:

> *I saw thy pulse's maddening play*
> *Wild send thee pleasure's devious way,*
> *Misled by fancy's meteor ray,*
>   *By passion driven;*
> *But yet the light that led astray*
>   *Was light from Heaven.*

God had given Burns his warm, generous and passionate nature, which—because it was undisciplined and uncontrolled —had led him, as he said himself, "into sin and folly". It would have been different for him if he had known sooner what it meant to accept the discipline of Jesus, Whose service is perfect freedom.

In spite of all the pressures which young people today have to face I am glad to see so many of them accepting the Christian standards. Chastity before marriage and fidelity after it are not outworn virtues. They may not be easy to maintain, but they are entirely possible for believing Christians. They are part of the secret of right relationships. They are stages in the apparently narrow way which leads, through Christ, to life in its fullness. He not only enables us to cope with life: He gives it to us more abundantly.

4

GROWTH TO MATURITY

IF I remember rightly, Bertrand Russell was once asked, "Do you believe in marriage?", to which he replied, "Of course I do. I have been married several times myself." This frivolous answer is typical of the attack which is being made today on the Christian view of marriage as a lifelong union between one man and one woman.

As a parish minister I have, on the average, thirty young couples who come during each year to make arrangements for their marriages. I try to see each couple at least three times before their marriage, discussing with them the details of the service, the meaning of Christian marriage and giving them—if they want it—information about books which may be helpful. I remind them that they could be just as legally married at a register office as in a church, but that there is a vast difference between the two ceremonies. A marriage before a registrar is a legal contract, but it may be broken by either party within the framework of the divorce laws. A marriage in a church is not meant to be broken at all. Christian marriage is for life.

This is not to say that all those who are married in a church live happily ever after. Sometimes their marriages fail and they are divorced. This is simply because their relationship is no longer that of Christian marriage. For one reason or another they turn to divorce. If they are Christians they can do this only because their relationship has so deteriorated that it is the lesser of two evils to be divorced than to keep up the pretence of a marriage that has ceased to be Christian.

The fact that the divorce rate in the United Kingdom has

stabilised at a figure of about 30,000 divorces each year shows that marriage as an institution is seriously threatened. There is no need to re-emphasise the sad results of this in so many areas of our national life. Broken homes mean unhappy people. This is one of the main reasons for the steady increase in the number of neurotics and juvenile delinquents. It has a great deal to do with the contemporary *malaise* in our society. If families cannot learn what it is to live happily together in their own homes, they will be ill-fitted to become useful citizens. The battle for the Christian home is fundamentally a battle for the health of the whole country.

I firmly believe that it is possible for any normal couple to keep the vows which are taken at the Christian marriage service, provided that they share the Christian Faith, and provided that they have a normal bond of affection for each other. A great deal is said about the difficulties of incompatibility of temperament. I am sure that G. K. Chesterton was right when he said that Christian marriage is based upon incompatibility of temperament. I have yet to meet any couple who are wholly compatible with each other. I should say that the vast majority of husbands and wives have a fair share of incompatibility. The successful marriages are those in which the partners have adjusted themselves to incompatibilities, or have learned to use them as complementary to what they themselves may lack. This process, of course, demands a steady and united effort which some people seem unwilling to give.

I think of many instances which I have known over the years, both in marriage guidance counselling and in parochial work. Here is a typical one. A woman who was obviously overwrought came to see me. Worried eyes, a lined face, trembling hands—she was in a bad way. Her marriage had a long history of tension and difficulty. Her husband was drinking heavily. He had gone to bed that afternoon, she said, for a drinking bout; and she was at the point of leaving him. She herself was getting tranquillisers from her doctor.

I called at the house. The door was unlatched and I went into the bedroom where the husband was in bed. He was perfectly sober, and we began to talk. I picked up some photographs lying on the floor. They were snapshots of his wife and his family—and a bonnie girl she had been when they were married. He admitted that for some time he had been drinking, and it was obvious that drink for him was the escape that tranquillisers were for his wife. It was equally clear that he had been—and still was—very fond of her. That was why the photographs were there.

At this stage his wife, who had now returned, burst into the room waving an empty bottle of pills, her eyes popping out of her head in anger. What she had not told me was that before she left the house that day her husband had put all the pills into his mouth and threatened to swallow them. He had, in fact, put them down the kitchen sink when she had gone out. His taunting scheme had been for her to come in, find the empty bottle, see him in bed and jump to the conclusion that he had taken an overdose. This was his way of getting his own back for what he called her "constant nagging". The whole situation was dismally pathetic, but it was by no means abnormal. Many happily-married couples have been too near to it themselves to be able to regard it scornfully.

I once heard an eminently respectable Scottish sheriff say that nine out of ten marriages come near to breaking point at one time or another. I believe this to be true. It can so easily happen that two people who are truly fond of each other find themselves involved in a quarrel in which they say and do things which they afterwards bitterly regret. I have had couples coming to see me who were terribly distressed by such an experience. They felt that there must be something abnormal and wrong in their relationship if this could happen. The fact that they were Christians only seemed to make it worse.

I have always tried to tell them that Christians, just as much as any others, can expect to find tension and difficulties in their marriages. Indeed there is a danger—and this applies particularly to the ministry—that people can become so busy in rushing about doing good works for others that they forget to pay enough attention to their own marriage relationship. It is when we are overtired that our defences against irritability and impatience are down, and we allow trivialities to swell into monstrous disagreements. But while this may happen, a shared Christianity can resolve the tensions and even lead to the marriage being enriched and strengthened because of them.

I mean this in no merely pious sense. I have little use for a religion which seeks to short-circuit practical problems by smarmy platitudes. It is because marriage is a demanding relationship that I believe it is worth while. It is because I know that men and women are imperfect that I am not surprised when I find that their romantic ideals are severely battered by their experience of marriage. It is because I believe that Christian marriage is God's way for men and women that I would defend it to the end as the means by which they can win through to true fulfilment.

I remember a well-known silversmith, Leslie Durbin, talking about his craft. It was when a splendid silver rose-bowl was being presented to Queen's College, St. Andrews University. The centre-piece of the bowl was a perfect little figure of St. Andrew, standing beside his cross. And as I heard Leslie Durbin speaking of the way in which he had fashioned the figure, I found myself thinking of the work of the Master Craftsman in the lives of men and women, not least in the marriage relationship.

Ignorant as I was about working with silver, I had thought of it as being hammered into shape. It is true that hammers are used, but Leslie Durbin made it plain that silver is a metal which has to be moulded and persuaded rather than bludgeoned. The craftsman deals with it almost as the potter deals with the clay, strongly but gently persuading it into the desired shape. Only so is the true potential of the metal realised.

In the making of men and women it is not force but persuasion that counts. This is the way in which God works with us. He does not hammer us into submission. He leaves us completely free. This is the kind of material that we are. If we are bludgeoned and beaten our true potential is lost. But we respond to the persuasion of the love of which St. Paul says, "Love is patient; love is kind and envies no one. Love is never boastful, nor conceited, nor rude; never selfish, not quick to take offence. Love keeps no score of wrongs; does not gloat over other men's sins, but delights in the truth. There is nothing love cannot face; there is no limit to its faith, its hope, and its endurance."

This is the way in which God loves us, and it is the way in which we must learn to love each other, above all in the relationship of marriage. If a man and woman have taken vows to each other, believing that they do so in God's presence, then whatever happens they can make up their minds that they will never break these vows. This gives their marriage an enduring stability. What will enrich it and make it the finest human relationship that anyone can know, will be their experience of the full meaning of love. They will treat each other as individual persons, because they know that this is how God treats them in the first place.

This is a long process which may involve setbacks and which needs patience. I have never been impressed by the attitude of some Christians which seems to imply that once you have made a "decision for Christ" you are a new being. To be sure, you may have made an important beginning, but you still have a long way to go. This came home to me all the more when I heard Leslie Durbin speaking about the making of the figure of St. Andrew.

A figure like this is not chiselled out of a block of silver, as a sculptor chisels a statue out of a solid block of marble. It is the result of a long, patient process. First there is the drawing of the craftsman's conception (in this instance it was based upon a painting of St. Andrew by El Greco); then there is a plasticine model, which can easily be altered; after that the figure is cast in wax and again in bronze, so that imperfections may be removed. Only when all this has been done is the final mould made, into which the pure silver is poured. All this, to make as perfect as possible the figure of a man in silver! "Take dross from silver," says the writer of the Book of Proverbs, "and the silver shines out pure."

There is good in every man and woman, a vein of pure silver. Surely the whole process of living in the world is designed by God to allow the dross to be taken away and the silver to shine out pure. This applies to all of us, whether we are married or single. I have always admired the men and women I have known who have remained unmarried and who have yet grown and developed into fine, mature characters. More often than not their fulfilment has been due to their Christianity and to their dedication to the work or cause in which their lives have been spent. I should never dream of denying that they were true men and women, any more than I should dream of denying full humanity to our Lord because He was not married.

At the same time it is clear that marriage is the fullest and best human relationship for the average person. And my contention is that its full purpose can be realised only by those who hold fast to it through thick and thin. Granted that second marriages after divorces may turn out well, this in no way lessens the Christian insistence upon marriage as being essentially the lasting relationship between one man and one woman. As is so often the case, what the critics denounce as another example of religious restriction is in fact divine commonsense. Maturity comes not through running away from difficulties through the divorce courts, but in facing them and overcoming them with God's help.

This can be a fascinating business, the very reverse of the

weary drudgery which is sometimes associated with the picture of a steady, enduring marriage. A craftsman making a figure of a man in silver has a lot of painstaking work to do, but he does not look on it as drudgery. He has the ideal towards which he is working, and there is a joy in what he does. In a much deeper sense there can be joy in dealing with marriage difficulties and adjustments. Instead of finding it merely irritating to be told frankly of one's faults by one's partner, one can learn to see this as worth while. It is by speaking the truth in love that we begin to grow up. We can reach the stage of coping with the faults in each other and helping to remedy them because we love the person in spite of, and along with, the faults.

If it is true that we find out the worst about each other when we are married, we can also—when we co-operate—bring the best out of each other too. We can find the pleasure of working together as a team, supplying what the other lacks, depending upon the other for something in which we ourselves are deficient. In all this we can discover so much that is interesting about human nature and about the whole business of living. And all the time we can be learning more about God, for it is in our closest human relationship that we find His reality.

This book is not a marriage manual. There are enough of them, in all conscience. But perhaps a plea can be made here for something which some such manuals seem too often to forget. Those of the secular kind concentrate especially upon the technicalities of the physical relationship. But no expertise in this field can by itself guarantee a happy marriage. Indeed it is of far more fundamental importance that even more intelligence and concentration should be devoted to the intricacies of mental and spiritual harmony than there is to the physical function. We happen to be made in such a way that the physical side of marriage can never be the full and liberating experience that it should be unless we are first in harmony with each other, and are treating each other as real persons. We have to get rid of the dross before the silver can shine out pure.

The aim of the Christian life is what Paul calls "mature manhood, measured by nothing less than the full stature of Christ". This is a high and challenging standard which some people feel to be far beyond them. But as I heard Leslie Durbin speak of how he had fashioned the silver figure of St. Andrew, I thought of how God had worked through Christ on Andrew, the rough and simple fisherman. Jesus saw the flaws in Andrew's character, but He also saw the man's true potential. He was always leading Andrew on from his failures to something better, replacing the imperfections with finer qualities. So at last Andrew, the apostle, missionary and martyr, was fashioned; the man who went to his death on a cross, but who asked that it might be a different shape from that of Jesus, because he thought himself unworthy of the upright Cross of his Master. This was growth to maturity.

Nor need we think that such growth is impossible for us. It is not that we can create it by ourselves. We need God's help for this, just as Andrew did. We need to believe that the Risen Christ is working in us in the whole of our lives. It can be a slow process, held back by our own selfishness and complacency. We need to see how God is leading us on through our experience of life. We are tested by difficulties; but if we overcome them we are a step farther on the road. We find other people painfully trying, but if we learn how to deal with them we have gained an inch or two of growth ourselves. What a mistake it is to think that Christianity is dull! It is always concerned with people and with relationships, and human beings are the most varied and fascinating material in all God's creation.

To find the interest and thrill of living like this we need a sense of purpose in it all. Leslie Durbin told us that he was sometimes asked what was the use of his craft and what he thought it achieved. His answer was a simple one, namely, that he sought to show the value of good craftsmanship, to create objects of beauty which would stand the test of time and would grow more lovely with use. It was a good and honest definition that he gave, and I could see that it derived from his own view of life as being something with a purpose.

It is precisely when the sense of purpose is lost that life becomes meaningless, "weary, stale, flat and unprofitable". If men feel like this about life then there is no conceivable reason why they should bother themselves about the words of Jesus, "You must therefore be all goodness just as your Heavenly Father is all good." Goodness in their view is something that Christians strive after through fear of hell or in the hope of a reward in heaven. They are intimidated or bribed into being good. This is not so. It would make nonsense of the lives of countless ordinary people, who have responded to the thrill of finding a purpose in living and who try to live the Christian life simply because they know it is worth while in itself. They realise that they can discover what Christianity means only when they try to put it into practice. In this sense it is like silver. The more it is used and tended the more brightly it shines, the better it becomes. It seems tarnished and useless only when it is left untouched. Use it, and go on using it, and it shines out gloriously; it will never wear away.

To have this sense of purpose is not only of value for the individual. It is also vitally necessary for the future of society. I become impatient with much of the theorising which goes on about alternatives to the Christian standards of home and family life and to the basic Christian rules of loving God and loving our neighbours as ourselves. Too much of it reminds me of fiddling when Rome is burning. We are faced with a situation in which, because people have lost a sense of purpose they are losing the place altogether, and have scant idea of how to live in right relationship with each other. They argue that they can retain the necessary values without the basis of Christian belief and apart from the Christian Church. But it is very plain that this does not happen. Once practice is separated from belief it steadily wears thinner, until it can completely disappear. I can think, for example, of three generations in a family I knew some time ago.

First came the great-granny, who was born in Victoria's reign. She knew all about the difficulties and tensions of life. She had had a tough upbringing in an industrial city with slums as bad as any in the country. Even when she was in her eighties she retained much of the beauty which must have glowed so vitally when she was a girl. One could see that she had always been as straight as a die. She had had her troubles—plenty of them—but she had brought up her family well. She had the Faith and she had the Church.

The next generation was rather different. They were nice people, but easy-going. I remember in particular the old lady's daughter, who herself had become a grandmother. She had drifted a bit both from the Faith and the Church. Late one night I had a telephone call telling me she was in trouble. When I reached her house I found her more distressed than I had ever seen any woman to be. She had been exceedingly proud of her son, but now it seemed that his whole life was going to pieces. His marriage was breaking up, he was away from his wife, he had become involved with another woman, he had started to drink, he was badly in debt—and all his troubles were pressing down on his mother's head.

Just because of the gradual slackening of the connection with the Faith and the Church, the third generation—the son and his wife—were even more out of touch. They had been married in church and had taken their vows, but they had ceased to see them as binding and had begun to lose their sense of purpose, just because they no longer worshipped together. They were not bad or vicious people. Like so many others they were essentially likeable and nice. It simply happened that because there was no inner compulsion to get to the root of the trouble between them, through love and forgiveness, they had not been able to break out of the vicious circle. The easy way out—which in fact was far more difficult in the long run—seemed to be to escape into unfaithfulness. Fortunately they saw this in time, and were re-united with each other and their children. But they had been on the brink of a situation in which so many people inevitably find themselves when they imagine that they can enjoy the fruits of Christianity without its roots.

I wondered, afterwards, how things would work out for them. In such cases it is advisable not to intrude after a reconciliation unless asked to do so. As it happened, however, I met the wife three years later. It was a moment or two before I recognized her and realised that she wished to tell me something. She said that she and her husband were living happily together, that their children were attending Sunday school, and that they themselves wished to renew their membership in the Church. They had found that they needed, at the deepest level of their relationship, the very things which had once seemed to be irrelevant.

When I visited their home and saw the children playing happily in it, I remembered vividly how different it had been three years before. The unhappiness and uncertainty had been replaced by peace and security. The family unit had been restored. The home was a centre of constructive living where previously it had been a house divided against itself.

The more I see of life in general and of marriage in particular, the more certain I become that Christianity is true, and that it is the foundation on which our personal relationships must be built. If a husband and a wife share a religious belief which they seek to put into practice and share with their children, they will be able to cope with whatever difficulties life may bring. They will find that their personalities are developed and enriched, and that as they grow closer to each other they come nearer to God.

5

HARVEST YEARS

IT is basic to Christian belief that life is not a mere meaningless struggle for existence but has a purpose. There is a pattern which works out in it, and this pattern is designed by God. We find this belief in the Bible, where we see God's purpose working out in the history of the Hebrews and in the lives of individual men and women. From this derives our confidence that He has a purpose for each one of us.

Admittedly it is not always easy to believe in such a purpose or to detect the design of a pattern. When we are involved in the daily bustle of our lives we are preoccupied with the immediate urgency of our problems or our difficulties. Like Martha we are anxious and troubled about many things. We find it difficult to be like Mary and choose the better part which leads to a clearer view of life as a whole.

There are times, however, when we can see more plainly how things work out. There are milestones at which we can pause, as it were, to look more objectively at the past and at the future.

To quote a personal experience, on a spring morning in 1964 my wife and I motored from Dundee to Glasgow. It was the anniversary of our silver wedding. On the way we passed Govan Old Parish Church where we had met when we worked together on George MacLeod's staff, and where we had been married. Our destination was a flat in the Gorbals where our elder daughter and her husband were working with the Gorbals Group (see Chapter III). Along with our other daughter and our son they had organised a celebration, the details of which had been carefully hidden from us.

As we made our way through the dilapidated entry and up the crumbling stairs, we wondered what surprises lay behind the door of the flat. Nothing could have pleased us more. In the room which was normally used as a children's play-centre our family had gathered twenty-seven of our relations and friends, some of whom we had never expected to see. They represented all the different stages in our lives. It was a very happy experience for us; and, as we both felt, it seemed entirely fitting that a marriage which began in Govan should have its twenty-fifth anniversary celebrated in the Gorbals.

This is a simple illustration of the way in which we can glimpse the pattern which God has been working out in our lives, and give thanks to Him for His Providence.

We can look back over the years behind us. They contain many mistakes and follies. Yet we can learn from our errors. Indeed it may be that because of them a richer pattern has been woven than might otherwise have been possible. It is good for us sometimes to be shamed and humiliated by the consequences of our actions. It brings us to ourselves. It makes us face up to what we really are. It points us to a new and better way.

As I look back from the middle years of life I am convinced of the reality of the moral law shown to us in Jesus. I have always clung to the belief that the moral law is no less real than the natural law, and that it is as foolish to disregard the one as it is to pay no heed to the other. A man may defy the law of gravity by walking over the edge of a precipice, but he cannot avoid the consequences. Similarly, if he flouts the law of love he will bring retribution on himself. It is not so much that God punishes him as that he inevitably becomes the victim of his own action.

Parents often tell me of their trouble and anxieties about their growing children, particularly in relation to the conflicting standards of home and the modern world. The youngsters complain about what seem to them to be old-fashioned restrictions. Their friends, they say, have much more freedom and less demanding standards of behaviour. As a result the parents are torn between condoning what they do not approve or (they fear) antagonising their children by taking a stand.

I have no hesitation in saying that the essential standards of Jesus should be resolutely kept in Christian homes. Life is a school of character, and it is in the home that the foundations of character are laid. By all means let us recognise that where the spirit of the Lord is, there is liberty. But if we believe that certain things are right and that others are wrong, we have an obligation to speak the truth in love to our children. We must be prepared to go through the wearing experience of reasoning it out with them and not evading issues just because it makes us uncomfortable to discuss them.

I am reasonably confident that when a lively sense of Christian standards has been instilled into young people, with love and understanding, there is every hope that they will carry on the same traditions when they have homes of their own. At my age I can see the children of our friends growing to manhood and womanhood. It is encouraging and inspiring to see so many of them following in the Christian way. To be sure, they give new expression to it. They by no means accept all the customs of their parents, some of which they can regard with an amused tolerance. On the basic issues, however, they stand firm, and to see them doing so is a great joy. This is the harvest of Christian character, which continues from one generation to another when Christ is honoured as Head of the home.

As I think of the enduring moral law I also think of God's Providence. I believe in Providence. That is why I look for a pattern in life and dare to think that I can trace it in my own experience. I cannot delude myself into imagining that God's Providence will care for me irrespective of what I do myself. It seems to me, rather, that only as I try to co-operate with Him can I find His Providence working out in my life.

Sometimes I have pictured life as a mighty stream, flowing

from God and returning to Him. I am launched on to this stream when I am born. I am carried along by it as the years pass. I cannot stop the momentum of life; I must go with it. Yet I am not without freedom of choice. It is as if I could guide the frail craft of my life in this direction or that as the stream flows on.

If I am wilful or foolish I may strike hidden rocks. I may be caught by wayward eddies. I may go aground on spits of sand, as it were, and lose the sense of progress. It is only as I use my freedom to follow in Christ's way that I can take my place in the mainstream of God's purpose and allow His Providence to work in me.

Any picture such as this is inadequate, but it may serve to express something of what can be felt in the middle years of life, when a man looks back and gives thanks for the way in which he has been led and guided thus far, in spite of all his mistakes and failures.

As we look back we also look forward. Some of us are growing older, fatter, balder and more scant of breath. Most are aware of old age creeping on, and perhaps the thought of our mortality blows chill around many hearts. We all fear the loss of dear ones and friends, the threat of loneliness and the gradual failing of our powers. Were it not for the Christian hope we might well give into a deep-rooted pessimism. Growing old could be a melancholy experience unless we shared the faith which says, "Though our outward humanity is in decay, yet day by day we are inwardly renewed."

It is because of this faith that we can come to see that character is the thing that matters most. It is something which can be enriched rather than defaced by the passing of the years. Thus one can meet old people who are frail in body but whose personalities are vital and inspiring.

I think of my wife's grandmother, now in her 102nd year. She is a remarkable person. She has all her faculties. She can still knit the most comfortable socks I have ever worn. After her hundredth birthday party, when she was on her way home, her companion suggested that she must be very tired and ready for bed. "Not at all," said great-granny, "I want to see the Black and White Minstrels on TV." And she did.

What I admire most in her is her sweet serenity. She has not had an easy or a sheltered life. When her husband was building up a one-man agricultural engineering business, she used to turn the lathe for him when her housework was done and her children were in bed. She wore old dresses so that new machinery could be bought. She has had her share of trouble and anxiety, but her face is calm and bright, with kindness shining from it. The reason is not far to seek. Throughout her whole life she has kept the Faith. She has lived not for herself but for God and for others. At the time of writing she is looking forward eagerly to the birth of our daughter's baby.[1] She knows that at any time she may slip away, but she is neither worried nor afraid. She has the Christian hope that death is not the end.

I know that she is an oustanding example (although not an isolated one), and that for many others old age brings grievous problems. The point, however, is that just as the Christian Faith enriches the blessings of old age so it enables people to cope with its difficulties.

Indeed I am never so certain of the reality of the Gospel as when I see it at work in many old people whom I have known. They could give points to the younger generation in their courage, vitality and humour. A number of the old women I know in Dundee began work as children in the jute mills for a weekly wage of a few shillings. Later they knew what it was to have their husbands unemployed when there was nothing but "parish assistance" which in their independence they abhorred. One would expect to find them embittered by their experience. On the contrary, their cheerful acceptance of all they have come through continually amazes me.

A typical example was one whose husband, while still a

[1] Susan (her first great-great-grandchild) arrived safely on 18th September, 1964.

young man, had been brought home a mangled wreck after a blasting accident at the quarry where he worked. Disabled, and totally blind, he never worked again, and sat in the house for thirty years before he died. At one time she had six children and £1 a week as her total income. When the situation became impossible she used to take a job in the mill, starting at six in the morning, until she had made enough extra money to buy boots and clothes. "The bairns," she used to say to me, "I kept going for the bairns. I couldna' give up." She lived for her family and she lived by faith in God. She never complained about life's hardness and she looked forward to its fulfilment after death.

There are others, of course, who crumple up under the onset of old age. We can be grateful that so much has been done in recent times to provide clubs and homes for old people and to improve the Dickensian institutions in which they were incarcerated. There remain, however, too many unhappy instances where practical Christian help and the communication of the Christian hope are needed. These provide a continuing opportunity for the Church. To meet this need in our congregation we have a team of seventy volunteers who regularly visit aged or infirm people.

There is, for example, the effect of loneliness. Late one evening a call came to our home from the Telephone Samaritans to say that someone my wife and I knew was at their office. She was a woman in her seventies who lived alone. Fear of a malignant disease had so preyed on her mind that she had gone out that night meaning to end her life. Fortunately she had gone to a police station in her distress and they had sent her to the Samaritans. She had been so ashamed of herself that she did not want to tell the minister. We took her home for the night, got in touch with her doctor and telephoned a relative in England. Treatment was arranged for her, and it was not long before she was able to come, with her Church visitor, to one of our old folks' outings, and feel that she was isolated no longer.

Added to loneliness there can be the loss of faith and lowering of standards. Character degenerates instead of becoming enriched. This happened with a woman who had worked hard at her job and nursed her invalid mother for eight years. After her mother's death and her own retirement she began to lose grip. When first I knew her it seemed as if nothing lay before her but a sordid alcoholism. It was almost impossible to get anywhere with her. When she was drunk she refused to open the door, and when she was sober she denied that she had been drunk. Both her outward appearance and her inward personality were in decay.

She was essentially such a nice person that one felt all the more sorry and frustrated at making no headway. The opportunity came when she was taken to hospital. She was surprised to be visited, but agreed to be put in touch with Alcoholics Anonymous and to have a visitor from the Church. A change was at once obvious both in herself and in her house. She began to take an interest in life. Previously she had tried to escape from it. Now she had discovered that there was a fellowship which cared. Qualities began to blossom in her which had been hidden for years. The real person could be seen emerging again.

It is in the context of such varied examples of character that I find myself thinking of the Christian belief in survival after death. Whether people are good or bad, fine characters or weak ones, they are all living souls. Why do we say that they live on after they die, and what do we mean when we say it?

Christians believe in the survival of personality because to believe otherwise would make nonsense of their belief in God. Once we start with belief in God, it is inconceivable to imagine that death is the end, that life is "a tale told by an idiot, full of sound and fury, signifying nothing." More than once I have stood beside people when they were in the actual moment of death. Instead of making me doubt in the afterlife this experience has made me the more certain of it. I could never bring myself to think of these persons ceasing to exist, like candles which had been snuffed out. It just would not make sense.

Nor does it make sense to imagine that our personalities are spongily absorbed by some infinite and impersonal consciousness. Christianity is not pantheism. It is based on the worth of the individual in the sight of God. As an individual I may be conscious of all my imperfections, but if I want to survive after death it is only as an individual that I shall find any meaning in survival. I may not be much of a person but I prefer continuing as a person to being submerged in a cosmic mathematical equation.

It is as well to make it clear at this stage that the Christian belief in the survival of personality is not dependent upon the activities of spiritualists, the evidence of extra-sensory perception or the transactions of the Society for Psychical Research. It is based upon the purpose of God in the creation of life and the Resurrection of Jesus Christ from the dead. The Christian belief is summed up in what the Apostles' Creed says about the resurrection of the body, the communion of saints and the life everlasting.

The resurrection of the body causes difficulty to many people. I can only testify what it means to me. It assures me that I can look forward to survival as a recognisable being. I need my body here on earth to express what I am as a person. In the Gospels I read that Our Lord appeared after His Resurrection in a recognisable and bodily form. At times it would seem that His body was spiritual, and again the implication is that it was physical, as when He broke bread with the disciples whom He met on the Emmaus road. I do not pretend to be able to explain this. I can only accept it, remembering that in the six weeks after the Resurrection He seems literally to have been moving between two worlds. What gives me confidence is that His disciples knew who He was. If I survive after death I expect to know others and to be known by them.

If, further, I am asked if I think that the remains of my

mortal body, whether it is buried or cremated, will be assembled together at the Final Judgment, I shall have to confess that I do not know. Nor indeed does my reading of 1 Corinthians 15 lead me to concentrate upon this as the fundamental issue. Rather do I turn to these words of St. Paul:

"But, you may ask, how are the dead raised? In what kind of body? A senseless question! ... What is sown in the earth as a perishable thing is raised imperishable. Sown in humiliation, it is raised in glory; sown in weakness, it is raised in power; sown as an animal body, it is raised as a spiritual body."

A Christian thus looks forward to individual survival. He does not, however, think of his future life as being lonely, as if he was to be an unhappy ghost straying solitary in an infinite void. He believes in the communion of saints, the fellowship of believers. The reality of life here is in fellowship, in meeting. It will be the same hereafter. He remembers what Jesus said about life after death, "Set your troubled hearts at rest. Trust in God always; trust also in me. There are many dwelling-places in my Father's house; if it were not so I should have told you; for I am going there on purpose to prepare a place for you. And if I go and prepare a place for you, I shall come again and receive you to myself, so that where I am you may be also."

However simple this belief may appear to the sophisticated and cynical, it is a faith which works. I have been impressed by the way in which, as people grow older, their experience confirms them in the basic Christian truths. I have talked with such people about death, and I have found them looking at it with level eyes. I have seen them calm and serene when their dear ones have died (and how different is the atmosphere in a house where there is no such belief!). They are not afraid of dying. They are not wandering into the unknown. They are following where Christ has gone before them. They are going home to God, to be with Him and those whom they love.

I remember quite clearly, as a boy, thinking about ever-lasting life and finding the prospect of it frightening rather than comforting. The thought of going on for ever made my mind reel and disturbed me. At that stage I had not realised that Jesus taught us to think of such life in terms of quality rather than quantity. Eternal life is the life abundant. It is what we can experience here and now, through Him, so that in this life we can have a foretaste of life hereafter. It is character that counts; and if we think of life in this world as a school of character we can believe that the process of learning will continue in the life beyond.

It has become too conventional a criticism to say that Christianity dangles the carrot of a heavenly reward before its followers. I do not find this to be the way in which Christians of my acquaintance look on the after-life. They believe in judgment, but, as Reinhold Niebuhr said some-where, they are not too concerned either about the furniture of heaven or the temperature of hell. They would agree with St. Paul that they will have their lives "laid open before the tribunal of Christ, where each must receive what is due to him for his conduct in the body, good or bad."

We brought nothing into this world and we can take nothing out. That is true, but only in the material sense. What we all take with us through death is character. The mere fact of dying makes no difference to the kind of persons we are. Thus if there are flaws and imperfections they will have to be remedied by training and discipline. If there are qualities of faith and leadership will they not be given a fuller and wider expression?

This is no cruel and inhuman doctrine. It is what we believe about the judgment of God, who is love. If we can see that in this world we are building for eternity we shall be all the more able to cope with life. We shall realise that we can-not escape the creative love from Whom our lives came and to Whom they must return. Nor, when we have come to be-lieve, should we ever wish to do so.

6

FACING UP TO LIFE

THE preceding chapters have outlined briefly something of what the Christian life can mean for an individual. In those which follow some wider issues will be considered. We cannot separate the appeal to the individual, with which the Gospel always begins, from his responsibility to play his part, as a Christian, in the problems of the world. Christ is to be seen both as the Saviour of men and as the Light of the world. If we see through Him that the love of God is the greatest power of all, we must believe that this power can be effective both in relationships between individuals and in relationships between nations.

The trouble is that both individuals and nations tend to regard love as a sentimental or irrelevant concept. How can they be brought to face up to life as Christians see it? How can they come to believe that love is the answer?

On the individual level, I recall a family in which relationships were awry, and there seemed little hope of putting them right. The husband was young, strong and in a good job, but the home was desperately unhappy. He was steadily drinking himself into alcoholism. He professed to be an atheist. He believed in exercising his authority as head of the house, but succeeded only in making himself and everyone else miserable. He was as tough as nails in resisting any approach. It was crystal clear that love was needed in that home, but he would have scoffed at it as a solution.

The time came, however, when he had to face up to himself. His drinking led to a serious illness. His wife came to see me and told me that although the doctors suspected the cause, he was trying to evade the issue. Together we agreed that the doctors must be told the truth, and that she should make every effort to persuade her husband to stay on in hospital and give himself a chance. As she said, "This is the only hope we have of finding happiness after all these years of misery."

I saw him when he was home for a few days from hospital. There was a difference in his attitude. He had made a real effort to come to terms with himself. He was staying on in hospital, and had begun to attend meetings of Alcoholics Anonymous.

"It's a queer, unfamiliar idea," he said. Of course it was. It meant that he had to take account of two things he had never taken seriously—spiritual power and human fellowship with others in the same need as himself. It was the beginning of his realisation that love could do something which he had not been able to do by himself.

As I write these words a letter from this man lies on my desk. He is still persevering with the new way. His wife is doing the same. She sees very clearly where things have gone wrong. She does not put all the blame on him, and admits her own responsibility. They both have a long way to go, but it is more hopeful for them than it has ever been before. They have faced up to themselves, and they see the relevance of love.

This is but one example of what has happened in innumerable instances in the history of Christianity. It proclaims that there is a separation between God and man caused by man's sin, and that in spite of this God continues to seek man in love —the love which He showed in the birth, life, death and resurrection of Jesus. This proclamation can be made in many ways, but it always demands a decision. The couple whom I have mentioned have had to face up to that decision. Either they accept or reject the reality of love. If they respond and go on seeking they will find that love is the answer. They will be saved from misery and unhappiness. By facing up to themselves they will have realised the need for personal responsibility.

Just because of the way in which great world issues are brought by TV, radio and the press daily into our homes, there has been a tendency to forget the personal responsibility of the individual to face up to himself. In a sense it is easier, and it can be a way of escape, to concentrate on issues like peace and war, racial discrimination, social justice, the hungry and under-privileged people of the world. That we should be concerned as Christians about all these issues goes without saying. They derive from what we believe about God and His love shown to us in Jesus Christ. The danger is that we should lose sight of the wholeness of His Gospel as applying both to individuals and to society. We must never so lose ourselves in these large issues that we forget that Christianity begins with our own personal responsibility as individuals.

Jean-Jacques Rousseau once said that his heart bled for humanity. An admirable sentiment—but he allowed his own children to go to an orphan institution. Charles Dickens had his Victorian readers weeping over the death of Little Nell —but his son said that the dream-children of the novels were more real to Dickens than his own flesh and blood. In the same way he idealized marriage in his autobiographical novel *David Copperfield*—but he broke up his own marriage by his association with an actress.

We cannot evade our personal responsibility. There is little sense in being idealistic about *apartheid* in South Africa or racial integration in America if we are guilty of social or intellectual snobbery in our own country. It is a pretentious mockery to talk about peace between the nations if we cannot live at peace in our families and with our neighbours. What is the point of waxing eloquent about social justice if we do not practise economic discipline in our own expenditure? We must face up to ourselves with integrity before we can stand on any pulpit or public platform to tell the world what it ought to do.

Thus as Christians we are aware of a constant tension between the individual and social implications of the Gospel. They cannot be separated. They are both parts of the same whole. The Gospel starts with the individual; but is Christianity merely a matter of the individual being "saved" into the good life? Will the world's problems be solved if a sufficient number of people become regular churchgoers? Even if this rosy prospect were to be realised there would be no guarantee that our Lord's prayer had been fulfilled when He said, "Thy kingdom come, Thy will be done, in earth as it is in heaven." It is becoming increasingly clear that Christianity is more than salvation for the individual. The whole world is the field in which love must work.

Thus on the one hand I see no answer to contemporary problems in the attitude which implies that young people are only "with it" if they have either marched to Aldermaston or lost their virginity. Along with our urgent concern that a nuclear holocaust should not devastate the world should go a determination to see that the kind of life which men lead in the world is worth preserving. Equally, however, no Christian today can justify an ostrich-like indifference to social and political issues while he pursues the even tenor of his way within the enclosed circle of the organised Church. If the love of God is the greatest of all powers it has to be seen as having a vital relevance in a world which is still overshadowed by the threat of nuclear war and of hunger. If in any real sense we are facing up to life we must face up to these things.

The difficulty is that we may be convinced of the reality of God's love in relation to individuals, but we may doubt if nations can ever come to see its relevance. Thus everybody agrees that we must work towards disarmament, but suspicion and mistrust prevent the first constructive steps being taken. Mankind is aware of the ultimate horror and absurdity of nuclear war. Willy-nilly the great nations are being shown that they must learn to love each other or die. They do not want to die, and they have not yet learned to love. But they know that they must do so. Either they set their faces to the painful but hopeful struggle towards interdependence and co-operation, or they resign themselves to the futility of destruction.

In a situation such as this Christians must of course be realistic. It does not help to sentimentalize about the theory of love. For my own part I have come to the conclusion that as far as the United Kingdom is concerned the way of love is the most realistic that we can take. I believe that we should abandon our so-called independent nuclear deterrent. I know that many fellow-Christians disagree with me, and they are entitled to their opinions. I can only state my own views, emphasising that they do not derive from membership in any political party, but from what I conceive to be the Christian attitude to this problem.

On the purely practical basis of argument it is obvious that any value in our possession of the nuclear deterrent is highly debatable. It is supposed to guarantee our presence at summit conferences, but we could be there whether we had the bomb or not. With the bomb, it is said, we have greater freedom of action than non-nuclear powers. This was certainly not apparent either at the time of Suez or in the Cuban crisis. For all the difference it made in these instances we might as well have been without it. It is more than doubtful if, for a small densely populated country such as ours, the bomb can have any military value whatsoever. It is quite certain that the money which is expended upon it could be used in far more useful ways, and that our possession of it is an encouragement to other non-nuclear powers to have bombs of their own.

I am not impressed by the argument which says, "The world knows Britain will not be the first to use it." The world still remembers the American bombing of Hiroshima and Nagasaki. I myself can recall the agonized discussion in Christian periodicals, during the first months of the Second World War, about limiting bombing to military targets. They had become terrifyingly academic by the time of the mass-bombing raids on Hamburg.

There is more than a suspicion that we are clinging to the bomb as a prestige symbol, a relic of the power of the British Empire upon which the sun never set. If this is so, does it bear any relationship to common sense or to Christian realism? We should be better to face up to ourselves, to realize that those days have gone for ever, and that our new rôle in world affairs must be entirely different. We have knowledge and experience to give to the world. We might even have moral leadership, but at the moment we appear to lack it. It would seem that having lost one conception of our destiny we have as yet failed to find another. We are wallowing in the trough of re-adjustment, and we are not going to be lifted out of it merely by material promises of an expanding and affluent society.

There are signs of hope on the world horizon, such as the Test Ban Treaty. Why I come down on the side of our abandoning the nuclear deterrent is that to do so would be a break in the present vicious circle. At the lowest level it could reasonably be argued that we should be no worse off. On another plane it would be a constructive step towards the kind of relationship with other nations which is so urgently needed.

To take this view does not mean adopting the complete pacifist position in recommending the immediate breaking of all military alliances and the disbanding of conventional forces. We may see the vision of a warless world, but we have to work towards it step by step. There is no political party in our country which would, in the foreseeable future, commit itself to a policy of total pacifism. Nevertheless there are signs of a growing body of opinion that our nuclear deterrent should go.

It may well be that many will disagree, even on Christian grounds, with this view. I can understand their attitude, although I cannot accept it. I hope, none the less, that they will agree that this is an issue which we must all face, as Christians, and that we cannot separate it from the implications of Christian belief in the love of God. The need still remains for us all to show its practical reality.

Perhaps one reason why we are uncertain about the power of love is that our minds are bemused by the signs of the power produced by scientific and technological means. When we see a massive power project such as a hydro-electric scheme, it is the skill and ingenuity of men that impress us most. They bore through solid rock, overcome tremendous obstacles, alter the whole appearance of the countryside and set up factories in the wilds. All this builds up in our minds so strong a picture of human power that we tend to forget that the whole project would be worthless but for one thing, namely the power of the water. Man is using his skill only to canalize the power which is there already and which he himself cannot create.

What men still lack, with all their scientific know-how, is the power to control and direct their achievements. Thus they have the knowledge and the means to solve the problem of world hunger. They still lack the power to break through the barriers of suspicion and fear which divide them from each other. The Christian Church has long been striving, not always with obvious success, to break through these barriers. In spite of all its inadequacies it has pioneered a way which the world will have to follow if mankind is to survive.

The Church, to be sure, is notably lacking in the kind of power exercised by governments. This does not really matter. When the Church had such material power and wealth it was spiritually at its weakest. Its real basis is belief in the power of God's love as the truly constructive and guiding principle for human life. Its task is to pioneer and show the example of what can be done, in however outwardly insignificant ways, in the power of love.

In relation to the vast problem of world hunger I think, to quote but one small instance, of what I saw in Jalna (see

Chapter II). It is a small outpost of Christianity, an apparently insignificant drop in the bucket of a continent where Christians form a tiny minority in a population of 450,000,000 people. An outside observer might dismiss it as irrelevant to the world issues which face us, but I believe he would be wrong.

The work that is being done in Jalna is, in microcosm, the work which needs to be done on a world scale, and with all the resources of human skill and knowledge. The material resources in Jalna may be scant, but they are being used in the spirit of love. There are little Christian congregations in the district. There is a mission hospital, which an Indian doctor told me was much more efficient than the government hospital. Work is being done with peasant farmers as one of the projects of the Scottish Committee for "War on Want." The Christian effort is being directed not merely towards individual "salvation" but towards wholeness in body, mind and spirit for those who are in need. There is an integration of preaching, healing and helping the hungry to help themselves.

The problem of under-nourishment broods over the Jalna area as it does over so many other under-privileged parts of the world. The peasant farmers need water to irrigate their small plots of land. Without such irrigation their fields grow crops which allow them only a marginal existence. When the crops fail, as they often do, villagers who might have worked on the fields are unemployed. Because they have no money to buy food, they and their children go hungry. Sometimes they die.

There is plenty of water underground, but ten feet down there is a layer of hard basalt rock which cannot be penetrated without mechanical aid and technical skill. This is where the "War on Want" project comes in. It is under the full-time direction of John MacLeod, a missionary who was an Inverness-shire farmer. The money from the supporters of "War on Want" is used by him to buy the necessary equipment and explosives. He has trained a team which goes round the district blasting the rock and digging and deepening wells for Christian and non-Christian farmers alike.

He described to me the difference this has made to one particular village where 500 people have their homes.

He and his team descended on the district to carry out an operation of digging thirty wells. They kept the equipment going on a 24-hour basis, and the noise of the explosions was like a veritable "blitz". But it was a blitz of love, not of bombs. The results were striking. This area had been sunk in a resigned apathy literally for centuries. Now new life was surging in. The Jalna Rotary Club, inspired by the project, had lent its aid in coping with government red-tape and bureaucratic forms. The people of the village rushed out in their enthusiasm to make a new road. The fields were irrigated. Crops of all kinds flourished in the soil. Seeds were actually exported to America. There was a new spirit of hope. Life was no longer a mere struggle for survival. And all because of the power of the Spirit working through human channels.

John MacLeod told me how one evening the local Income Tax Inspector came to see him. "Tell me," he said, "why do you come here to do this kind of work? I suppose it must be your religion. I myself am a Hindu, but I do not believe in my religion any longer. Yet I can see that unless men believe in a spiritual power there can be no solution to the world's problems." There is the matter in a nutshell. It is at once the reason why Christians must go on pioneering and the hope that their efforts are not in vain.

If we are aware of our personal responsibility, surely such responsibility extends to those who are hungry and under-privileged. Wherever in the world they are they belong to the human family. They are our brothers and sisters. We have an opportunity of expressing our love towards them in the most practical way.

When I was in Australia a lady heard me speaking about Jalna. She was interested and wanted to help. Her way of doing so was to buy oil shares in a Queensland project and hand them over to John MacLeod. Thus, if they strike oil in Queensland it will mean more water in Jalna, thousands of miles away.

In our own congregation, as an additional Stewardship effort, we have decided to support the Jalna work. In two years we have raised nearly £700, and our aim is to raise £1,000 to pay for a tractor.

Of course these are tiny efforts, but they matter. They form a chain of interest and concern which spans the world. They are expressions of the love which should bind us all together. However small they may seem, they are channels which God can use, they are means of dispelling the frustration and apathy we can experience in the face of world problems.

A doctor once told me of a case which illustrates this point. A colleague had spoken to him of a lady who was afflicted by a curious *malaise* which seemed to defy diagnosis. She had no outward symptoms of illness. She was eating and sleeping normally. Yet she continued to feel unwell.

The doctor decided that at least he should sound her. The moment he applied his stethoscope he received a severe electric shock. The reason was that she was clad entirely in nylon—and her shoes had rubber soles. All the static electricity created by friction against her nylon clothing was surging about in her body, unable to earth itself because of the insulation of the rubber.

Here is a parable for frustrated Christians. Too often such frustration can be due to the way in which our souls are insulated against the power of love. We know all about it in theory. We absorb the idea of it from sermons and from books. It becomes real and effective, however, only when we express it in what we are and in what we do. It has to be earthed, flowing out to meet the problems and difficulties of life.

If in any real sense we face up to life we must face up to our own personal responsibility. The issue is not what others are doing or failing to do, but what we ourselves are doing. This was what Peter learned from Jesus beside the sea of Tiberias, after the Resurrection. Peter was concerned about Jesus' plans for John. But Jesus said, "If it be my will that he wait until I come, what is it to you? Follow me." This is the beginning from which all else should come. Only as we follow in His footsteps do we find the way to cope with life.

7

A QUESTION OF FAITH

THERE is little meaning in talking about personal responsibility unless we have a sense of being personally responsible to someone. I have heard agnostic existentialists of the Sartre school of thought speaking about the need to be personally responsible. But to whom are they responsible? Not to God, because they reject the idea of a supernatural being. To other people? But Sartre has said, "Hell is other people", which seems to run counter to recognising our responsibility to do to them as we would that they should do to us. Are we then to be responsible only to ourselves? In that event, we make our own standards and values and do exactly as we choose—which brings us back to where we were before.

The traditional Christian teaching is that we are personally responsible to God and to our neighbours. I can see no good reason for departing from this belief. The Bishop of Woolwich in *Honest to God* seems to show rather a surprising sympathy with Sir Julian Huxley's statement, "For my own part, the sense of spiritual relief which comes from rejecting the idea of God as a supernatural being is enormous." I can understand Sir Julian Huxley's sense of relief, but I have no desire to share it.

I can see that it may be a nuisance to feel that there is a Person who is concerned about the way in which I behave and to Whom I am responsible for my behaviour. Equally it could appear to be a nuisance that there should be certain unchanging and absolute values by which I am obliged to regulate my actions. But if this is a nuisance, I am prepared to accept it as a condition of being a Christian. I have in any event to accept, like all other people, certain standards and ideals in many other spheres. An artist has in his mind an ideal towards which he is working in the picture which he is painting. So has a cook or an engineer, a writer or an actor, a poet or a dressmaker. Anyone who wishes to do a thing well has to learn the necessary rules of the craft, trade or profession in which he is engaged. In the over-all business of living I know that I must accept some standards and also some restrictions. I prefer taking them from God as shown to me by Jesus Christ, to taking them from Sir Julian Huxley or anyone else who tries to maintain that there is no supernatural being and no absolute standard of values.

The Bishop of Woolwich seems to be over-anxious to dispose of the image of the God "up there" or "out there". In contrast, he wants us to think of the God "down there", of God as being "in depth". This is really a question of replacing one image or conception of God by another. Instead of climbing, the Bishop goes in for pot-holing. Or in more theological terms, he is uneasy about the transcendence of God and wishes to emphasise His immanence.

I cannot see that all the Bishop has said so sincerely makes much difference to the Christian position. I get the impression that he is desperately anxious to make traditional Christian belief acceptable to modern men, particularly to unbelievers. This is extremely laudable, but to my mind he falls between two stools. He worries a great many simple Christians (which may not necessarily be a bad thing if it makes them review their beliefs more seriously) by giving them the impression that he has thrown out the baby with the bath water. In fact, after various explorations, he usually surfaces to a semi-orthodox belief.

On the other hand, he holds out an accommodating welcome to the agnostics, saying in effect, "You really are believers without knowing it. Why don't you come in and join us?" But to this, as Miss Marghanita Laski has made plain, their answer is apt to be "Not on your life! If you really feel like that, why don't *you* come and join *us*?"

For my own part I find it better (because it appears to me to be incontrovertible) to accept the fact that the essentials of Christian belief will always be a stumbling block and foolishness to the agnostics as they were to the Jews and the Greeks 1,900 years ago. I am prepared to defend my beliefs in argument but I do not normally expect to argue anyone into following Jesus. Argument tends to remain on the surface level without touching sufficiently the deeper springs of human personality. It is necessary, but it is not enough.

I read from time to time what the agnostics have to say. Their cleverness impresses me. They seem to know all the answers, but I wonder if they make it all sound too easy. I do not know all the answers. Indeed I am glad that I don't.

When an agnostic says that human life is the product of the accidental collocation of atoms, and derides the Christian doctrine of creation, I seem to hear an echo of the immortal words of Pooh-Bah in *The Mikado*, "I am, in point of fact, a particularly haughty and exclusive person, of pre-Adamite ancestral descent. You will understand this when I tell you that I can trace my ancestry back to a protoplasmal primordial atomic globule. Consequently, my family pride is something inconceivable. I can't help it. I was born sneering."

The kind of world which the agnostic view pictures is marvellously rational, scientific and hygienic, mechanised by automation and controlled by electronic brains. It is staggering—and it is appalling. It is excessively modern—and it is unspeakably dull. It would take all the mystery and wonder out of living. It by-passes the fundamental questions, "Why am I here? What am I to do? Where am I going?", or simply gives the dusty answer that everything has to be explained in terms of sense-perception. A Christian cannot accept this view. He may not be able to argue as convincingly as the agnostic, but intuitively he knows that the agnostic is wrong. Christianity has never pretended to give all the answers to all the questions. It does, however, give a clue to living which enables people to see a purpose by which they may live and a Person Whom they can follow.

There are, of course, some questions which agnosticism seems to answer far less satisfactorily than does Christianity. I cannot accept the belief that the world and human life exist by accident. It is quite unreasonable to believe that a purely mechanical universe has produced something greater than itself, namely the human mind. I see in materialism no explanation of the undoubted existence of a sense of right and wrong.

I think there is far more reasonableness in the Christian explanations, and I fully agree with G. K. Chesterton when he said that his faith had been confirmed by reading the arguments of the nineteenth century scientific materialists. Sir Julian Huxley has the same effect on me when I read his description of what he calls the religion of evolution. He would retain the apparatus of religion—prayers, temples and all—without its content. This is a dreary prospect, and I am certain that temples of evolution, if they ever came into being, would remain fittingly empty.

In any event, anyone who stands outside of Christianity cannot really direct any final and irrefutable argument against it. I like the limerick which refers to Professor A. J. Ayer's logical positivism as follows:

> There was a young man who said, "Ayer
> Has answered the atheist's prayer.
>   For a Hell you can't verify
>   Surely won't terrify—
> At least till you find that you're there."

The proof of the pudding is in the eating of it, and the only proof of Christianity that is finally valid is to be found in the living of it. M. Sartre, rejecting the supernatural, says, "Hell is other people." Christians, retaining the supernatural, know that hell is separation from God and from other people.

By the same token they know that the reality of heaven is to be found in harmony with God and with their neighbours. Argument on the theory of the supernatural, and of heaven and hell, can go on indefinitely. It is only when one starts to apply the theory in practice that the knowledge, which is based on experience, comes.

This is the one thing which an agnostic, no matter how sympathetic he may be towards certain aspects of Christianity, cannot find by directing a dispassionate gaze towards it. This was obvious in the witty and entertaining film *Heavens Above!* made by the Boulting brothers. It contained some shrewd thrusts against organised religion, thrusts which must have had a traumatic effect upon many ecclesiastics and church members. But because it was conceived from a standpoint outside of the Christian Church it made some fundamental mistakes.

No one in his senses could imagine that the local Lady Bountiful in the film was acting in a Christian way when she organised a free distribution scheme which deprived the local shopkeepers of their trade. The Boulting brothers seem to have forgotten that it was St. Paul and not Karl Marx who first said, "The man who will not work shall not eat." If this is their view of Christianity it is not surprising that they should come to the conclusion that it is entirely impracticable on earth, and send their likeable little vicar off to be the Bishop of Outer Space.

Anyone who was writing a film from within the Church could never limit it with the title "Heavens Above!" By implication this is nothing more than the old idea of the Epicurean philosophers that the gods led a remote existence beyond the clouds, caring nothing for what happened on earth. Those who worshipped them did not expect the gods to have any radical effect upon human behaviour, apart from the regular offering of placatory sacrifices. The Christian title of any film would have to be something like "Down to Earth!", for this is the basis of our belief, namely, that the supernatural and transcendent God is incarnate and immanent in Jesus Christ; that He is to be found and known through Christ, through other people and through the everyday living of the Christian life.

This same misunderstanding of Christianity is evident in Julian Huxley's introductory essay in the collection of humanist writings edited by him under the title *The Humanist Frame*. In one illuminating sentence he says, "Evolutionary man can no longer take refuge from his loneliness by creeping for shelter into the arms of a divinized father-figure whom he has himself created, nor escape from the responsibility of making decisions by sheltering under the umbrella of Divine Authority, nor absolve himself from the hard task of meeting his present problems and planning his future by relying on the will of an omniscient but unfortunately inscrutable Providence."

One has to take these words at their face value. This is what Sir Julian Huxley imagines religion (and presumably the Christian religion) to be. I can only say that this is not what I was taught by anyone, it is not my experience of religion, and it is not what I have seen it to be in the view of Christians I have known. This definition carries overtones of Freudian jargon and nineteenth century scientific materialism, neither of which has any permanent authority; and one of the best ways in which I can test its validity is simply to measure it against some examples of ordinary Christian people I have known.

When, for example, I read that religion for man is to "take refuge from his loneliness by creeping for shelter into the arms of a divinized father-figure whom he has himself created", I think of a little lady whom I met in Brisbane. St. Andrew's Church, where I was guest preacher, ran a "Meals on Wheels" service as part of their Christian Stewardship. My wife and I went round with two of the team of helpers, and one of our calls was on this lady, who was 86 years old. Like so many others in Queensland, her roots were in Scotland, and when we met her she was reading the life of a well-known Scottish minister, Robert Murray McCheyne, who had a notable ministry in Dundee in the early nineteenth century. It was a coincidence that I also came from Dundee, and that it was due to the influence of McCheyne that my grandfather had decided to study for the ministry over a hundred years ago. But apart from that I could have met few better examples than that of this gallant lady to give the lie direct to Huxley's definition of religion.

For one thing, her family tradition was quite the reverse of creeping into an escapist bolt-hole. Her grandfather had been a crofter in Shetland in the days when the Shetlanders suffered from the extraordinarily ruthless oppression of the local lairds. These islands were so far away from the centre of government that no one seemed to realise that feudalism still persisted, through and beyond the Industrial Revolution farther south. In the Shetland tradition her father had gone to sea, and had sailed twice round the world before he was twenty-one. From Australia he wrote to his family saying that here was a country where they could make a life for themselves; and after his parents set sail on the six-months' voyage, he walked the 500 miles from Sydney to Melbourne to meet them. This was the way of many of the early migrants to Australia. They had courage and they had faith. Ask any of their descendants today if they were creeping for refuge into the arms of a divinized father-figure, and I can imagine the direct and blistering answer that will be given!

As religion had been the foundation of the family life in Scotland, so it was in Australia. For the greater part of her life this lady had been caring for a son who suffered from a distressing mental handicap. When we met her she was rarely able to leave him in the care of anyone else. Of course she found a refuge in God, but God was also her strength. She had never tried to escape from life. She met it bravely, taking everything that came, never complaining or cringing, always looking outward, urgent in her concern for spreading the Christian message.

Later she came to see us in our hotel, and it was a refreshing and invigorating experience to talk with so vital a person. It would have done Sir Julian Huxley good to meet her. Perhaps it is because he does not realise what ordinary Christians are like, and what in fact they believe, that he allows himself the luxury of caricaturing their faith.

When, further, it is said that evolutionary man, having discarded religion, cannot "escape from the responsibility of making decisions by sheltering under the umbrella of Divine Authority" one wonders where to look for examples of this kind of religion. I should have thought that for the average Christian his acceptance of Divine Authority would constantly be presenting him with decisions which he felt he had a responsibility to take, hard and uncomfortable though they might be.

If he is a business man he knows that he has a responsibility not to fiddle his expense account. If he is an employer he feels a duty to give his workers just wages and conditions. If he is an industrial worker he is aware of an obligation to put in an honest day's work in return for his pay. In all such instances his religion is not a means of evading decisions. It is, in fact, because of Divine Authority that he is compelled to face up to them.

Conversely, it would seem reasonable to expect an agnostic to be less likely to face up to decisions, precisely because he rejected the responsibility of obedience to any supernatural being. It would be easy to quote examples of saints and reformers who disproved Huxley's assertion, but as they might be regarded as exceptional I prefer to think of the people whom I have met in the course of my work as a parish minister. They would not class themselves as exceptional. They were simply people who believed in trying to find God's will and put it into practice.

I think of men who have decided, often at no small cost to

themselves, to enter the Christian ministry. I know several who have given up good positions in business to do this. It has meant for some men a drastic cut in income, a lower standard of living for their wives and children, and going back to years of study. I remember an Australian who decided during war service to study for the ministry. He had to take all his higher education after the war, when he was a grown man. He had to face being down to his last few pounds of capital, and go through the trial of wondering if it was fair to his wife and children to carry on. Such decisions are the inevitable result of Christian obedience, and those who take them do not find it easy either to make them or to follow them through.

Similarly, I fail to understand how the normal Christian could be said to "absolve himself from the hard task of meeting his present problems and planning his future by relying on the will of an omniscient but unfortunately inscrutable Providence." This is an obvious, if typical, misunderstanding of the Christian belief in the Providence of God. It is really a better definition of the non-religious attitude to Fate or Chance, where men lapse into indifference because they think that whatever they do is immaterial in face of the inscrutable working of Fate. A belief in Providence implies a belief in the purpose and meaning of life. It further implies that this purpose can be found only by active co-operation with God's Providence. It can never be a matter of leaving everything to Him. We must be fellow-workers with God.

If we hold to this belief it certainly does not absolve us from meeting our problems or planning our future. It should mean that we are better able to meet our problems because we shall try to solve them in the Christian way. We ought to be able to plan our future with more confidence and less worry if we try to follow Christian principles. We know that the future is in God's hands and that the only way in which we can meet it is by doing what is right in the present. We do not live in the future any more than we live in the past. When Jesus said "Do not be anxious about to-morrow" He was not telling us to be improvident or to leave everything to God. He was telling us to do the right in the here and now, knowing that as we do so we are making the only satisfactory preparation for the future.

I have seen this Faith tested in the most bitter and tragic way and survive triumphantly. Once I was asked to take private Communion to an invalid. She was a doctor's wife in an Australian suburb. A few years earlier life had seemed wonderful. She was young and beautiful, happily married and with a small daughter. Now she was the victim of a painful and disfiguring illness which kept her in bed, although she could with great difficulty struggle up sometimes to do some domestic chores.

To celebrate the Sacrament in her room was a high privilege and a deeply moving experience for me. There was no bitterness, no sadness. She was meeting her problems. She spoke to her husband's patients when they telephoned their troubles and anxieties. She was training her young daughter (still a schoolgirl) to take her place. Perhaps she could not understand why her sickness had to happen—and indeed who could understand?—but she accepted it and coped with it without flinching. In what could so easily have been a sad and gloomy situation there was a bright gladness which was real and tangible. The future seemed dark, but because God was in the present there was nothing to fear. As her husband said to me, "We did not want this to happen. But because of it we have come to know God and each other in a way which would not have been possible otherwise."

Afterwards I wrote to her and asked if sometime I might tell her story in order to help others to understand the Christian way. Back came a note giving her willing permission, and with it a bunch of violets for my wife. On the accompanying card were written the words, "Till we meet again." We were leaving Australia, and she knew that we should not see her before we left. But she was not thinking in terms of this life;

and that, I am sure, is the reason why the Faith is at once foolishness to the agnostics and impervious to all their slick criticisms of it. It is the victory which overcomes the world. They may attack it as they will, but they cannot disprove it.

Christians should have no hesitation in saying this as frankly as they may. After a debate in which I had been defending the Christian position I was taken to task by my agnostic opponent for "being so rude" about his views. He seemed to expect that, as a Christian, I should not indulge in the kind of remarks which he made about my beliefs and the Christian Church of which I was a representative.

I had to point out that there was a clear distinction between loving one's neighbour as a person and being nice about the opinions which he held. There is no Scriptural precedent for being kindly disposed towards misrepresentations of the Gospel. Nor are we showing our love and compassion towards unbelievers if we seek to share their unbelief with them. We can indeed show that we have known what it is to stand on the borders of unbelief ourselves. But what will help them is not that we should share in their agnosticism but that we should communicate to them those things of which, amid all the uncertainty of human existence, our experience has led us to be convinced.

This is a more urgent task than is sometimes realised, just because the agnostic and Christian views of man are so radically different. This was brought home to me as I viewed a transmission of the BBC Brains Trust when the panel was composed of Dr. Bronowski, Dr. Alan Bullock and Professor A. J. Ayer, all of whom rejected the Christian position. A questioner had asked what arguments the Brains Trust could give against the vivisection of prisoners by Nazi doctors in concentration camps in the Second World War. The Brains Trust naturally deplored such practices, but there was nothing fundamental in what anyone had to say.

The Christian answer to the question would have been simple and final. The value of the individual human being does not lie in the fact that he has appeared at the summit of an age-long process of evolution. His eternal significance is due to the fact that God loves him and Christ died for him. The sin of the Nazi doctors was due to their disregard of the twin laws of love of God and love of neighbour. When these laws are rejected, anything can happen and anything can be justified, because man is then personally responsible to no one but himself.

In May, 1964, a libel case was heard in which Dr. Wladyslaw Dering sued the publishers of *Exodus* by Leon Uris, in which it had been alleged that Dering had carried out such operations at Auschwitz. He claimed that he had acted under threat of death; and the jury awarded him damages of one halfpenny.

It is significant, however, that another doctor imprisoned at Auschwitz refused to perform similar operations. Her name was Dr. Adelaine Hautval. She was a devout French Protestant, the daughter of a Reformed pastor. Her refusal was based on her religious belief. An SS doctor had asked her if she could not see that the patients they were dealing with were Jews and therefore different from her. Dr. Hautval's reply to the Nazi was that she saw she was different from him. And we can see why. She was personally responsible to God and to her neighbour.

The keystone of agnostic humanism is its belief in the self-sufficiency of man. So far from being a strength, this is its real weakness. Life has a habit of showing up man's attempts at self-sufficiency.

Inevitably there come the times when we are stripped of our material (but ephemeral) defences, and stand as naked souls before the mystery and tragedy of existence. An agnostic deserves not scorn but compassion in such circumstances. On his own admission he is alone, and there is none to help him.

A Christian knows that he is not alone. He may not see the way ahead clearly, but he still can trust. He may not be able fully to understand, but he still believes. He knows from experience that time and again he has had to say, "Lord, I can't do this by myself. Please help me." By admitting his weakness he has found strength. He has proved that he can begin to cope with life only when he acknowledges his dependence upon a power greater than himself.

8

YOUR ENEMY THE DEVIL

IN our coping with life we inevitably come up against the problem of evil. We may make bold assertions of our belief in God, but our belief is no bland optimism which discounts the inescapable fact of human sin. It is interesting to note that humanists seem in this respect to be less realistic than Christians. They project a surprisingly rosy picture of evolutionary progress in which man is the master of all things. They grow hot under the collar at the mention of original sin. But they cannot deny the fact that there is a curious imperfection in human nature which has the most disturbing results. To be sure, they do their best to explain it away. They do not call it sin. They attribute it to defects in the individual's early upbringing or environment. They say that it can be dealt with by psychological treatment and enlightened educational methods. And so on. But the facts are too uncomfortably real. Whether one considers the criminal statistics or the general picture of man's inhumanity to man, evil is seen to be constantly at work.

It would be foolish to imply that there is any easy answer to the question why there should be evil in a world which we believe the good Lord to have created. It is also foolish to reject the clues which the traditional Christian position provides. The Christian view of man is not popular in an age when man thinks highly of himself and his achievements. That it is unpopular matters less than that it should be seen to be both realistic and true.

In a TV programme called *Your Adversary The Devil* I made an attempt to say something about the problem of evil.

For the purpose of visual illustration there were in the studio some photographic enlargements of various devilish characters. One of these was da Vinci's "Prince of Hell". During the rehearsal an inexperienced caption operator got his captions in the wrong order. The result was that just at the point where the Prince of Hell was shown glowering from the monitor screen, the caption superimposed on the picture read, "The Rev. Dr. Hugh Douglas". This was a source of innocent merriment in the studio. But afterwards, when I was visiting a lady who had viewed the transmission of the programme, and told her of the mistake in rehearsal, her comment was, "To tell you the truth, I thought the picture was rather like you."

This was scarcely a flattering remark, but perhaps there was more truth in it than the good lady realised. In traditional Christian language, there is something of the devil in us all. St. Paul puts it this way, "The good which I want to do, I fail to do; but what I do is the wrong which is against my will." In more contemporary terms, Studdart Kennedy put the same thought in the language of a soldier:

> There's nothing in man that's perfect,
>   And nothing that's all complete;
> 'E's nubbat a big beginning,
>   From 'is 'ead to the soles of 'is feet.
> There's summat as draws 'im uppards,
>   And summat as drags 'im down,
> And the consekence is, 'e wobbles
>   'Twixt muck and a golden crown.

And St. Peter gave the idea colourful expression by writing, "Awake! be on the alert! Your enemy the devil, like a roaring lion, prowls round looking for someone to devour."

It is fashionable, of course, to regard the devil as an outworn concept. I have in my study a copy of *Pilgrim's Progress* which was given by my grandfather a hundred years ago to one of my uncles. In it there is a lurid picture of the foul fiend attacking Christian in the Valley of the Shadow of Death. One can smile at it as a typical example of Victorian religiosity. Christian looks almost too good—or too pious—to be true; and Apollyon is made to appear so horrifying as to excite laughter rather than dread. This, one imagines, is the concept of the devil from which enlightened twentieth-century man believes himself to have been emancipated.

There was a time when I should probably have accepted this sceptical view of the devil. The climate of opinion in which I grew up was strongly influenced by the discoveries of science and psychology. One was inclined to regard the devil as a picturesque allegory, rather in the category of the demon king in a pantomime. One doubted if it was intellectually respectable to believe in his existence. Now I am much more inclined to take the devil seriously, simply because experience of life brings with it experience of the active power of evil.

Admittedly any picture of the devil must be put in mythical form, and there is a school of thought which seeks to sweep away the myths of the Bible as obstacles in our search for truth. This is done, presumably, in the cause of scientific accuracy. But one cannot so easily dispose of the biblical myths, which can be seen as valid channels for conveying religious truth. It is odd to see how they can be dismissed as fairy tales when at the same time pagan myths are given the status of intellectual respectability.

Freud, for example, took the myth of Oedipus as an illustration of his theory of infantile sexuality. He went so far as to say that "every new arrival on this planet is faced with the task of mastering the Oedipus complex". As he told Jung, he wished to make a dogma out of his belief that repressed sexuality was the root cause of human ills. If we are to have dogmas, let us have better ones than this, and such as really have a universal application. There is a fundamental truth in the biblical myth of the Garden of Eden which is lacking in Freud's application of the Oedipus story. The Bible provides a much more satisfactory explanation of the existence and nature of evil.

We cannot believe that God creates both good and evil, nor that God creates good while some equal and independent power creates evil. The traditional Christian teaching is that God is the Creator and that freedom of choice belongs to all whom He has created. The Garden of Eden story tells us that through pride and disobedience man misuses his freedom. He says that he does not need God to show him what to do, and he eats the fruit of the tree of the knowledge of good and evil. He knows then—as we all know—what is wrong, and he still goes on choosing it. Man wants to be equal with God, and so he pretends to be a god himself. The implication behind the story is that the Fall of man through pride and disobedience was preceded by the Fall of some subsidiary and supernatural power through the same pride and disobedience.

The Garden of Eden story, incidentally, does not imply that the sex-instinct is sinful. On the contrary, it shows that the right functioning of the instinct within the law of God (that is, within marriage) is good, but that its functioning outside of marriage is wrong and shameful. The story deserves much more careful study than it receives.

To believe in evil as an active power does not mean that we have to picture the devil as he was shown in the old edition of *Pilgrim's Progress*. It does mean that we have to recognise the fact that our Lord believed in the existence of a personal evil power. This is made very clear in the first three Gospels, is confirmed in a slightly different way by the fourth Gospel, and is followed by St. Paul in several of his letters. The story of the Temptation in the wilderness shows us the reality of the struggle with evil which Jesus endured. It is all very well to say that He accepted the thought-forms of His time, but exactly the same could be said about His belief in the existence of God. It cannot be denied that Jesus believed in a personal devil any more than it can be denied that He believed in a personal God.

When we read the Gospels, however, we do not find in them speculative theories about why there should be an evil power at work in the world. We find a remedy for sin. We see that this was the prime purpose of Jesus Himself. He was called "Jesus" or "Saviour" because He was to save His people from their sins. When He began His ministry in Galilee, His first word was "Repent", which means "Change your hearts. Turn from yourselves and your sins to God. Make a new beginning".

One finds this purpose running through everything that Jesus said and did. This emphasis did not make Him a gloomy, puritanical kill-joy. Rather does it show Him as the Great Physician, come to deal with and to cure a fundamental sickness in the lives of men. Just as disease disintegrates the health and wholeness of the body, so sin does this to the human personality. Because sin is pride and disobedience to God, it conflicts with God's good purpose. Jesus came to remedy this. The salvation which He gives is not a pious phrase, but a glorious reality. It is the saving from disintegration. It is the restoration of integrity and wholeness. It is true health.

If health is to be restored, there must first be a diagnosis of the nature of the disease. I am forced to take the disease of sin seriously because I come up against it every day in my own life and in the lives of other people. If I want it dealt with I must try to see first what precisely is wrong, and then what the remedy of the Great Physician is.

There is an ancient classification of the Seven Deadly Sins as Pride, Wrath, Envy, Avarice, Sloth, Lust and Gluttony. This in itself makes it plain that Christianity does not concentrate, as is sometimes supposed, on the sins of the flesh like drunkenness and sexual immorality. Nowadays, in fact, it is customary to point out that Jesus condemned the sins of the spirit more severely than the sins of the flesh. But there is a danger in such a division. It is more true to say that all sin begins in the spirit. No sin was ever condoned by Jesus, and no sinner who was repentant was ever turned away by Him. He would not necessarily be more lenient to an alcoholic than to a proud hypocrite or to an adulterer than to a malicious gossip. His concern would be to heal them all rather than to assess the degree of their sinfulness.

It is true that Jesus did not seem to be preoccupied with the sins of the flesh to the extent that some of His followers have been, but He had some very straight and uncomfortable things to say about them. Nor could it be true to His spirit ever to imply that, for example, sexual immorality really does not matter. We recognise that a man is committing wrong in stealing £10,000 in an armed bank robbery. Is he any worse than a man who steals another man's wife and gets away with it? We are indignant with the cosh-boy who beats up a girl and takes her hand-bag. Is he more of a sinner than the cultivated young man who, after a riotous party, seduces a girl whom he has met for the first time, never bothers to see her again and leaves her to endure the mental agony of finding herself pregnant and bearing his child in illegitimacy? We are concerned about the standards of integrity in public life. Is there any reason why a philanderer or an adulterer should be rated on a higher level than a thief? If we are looking for integrity and wholeness we must look for them everywhere, and if there is something unsound in one part, then the whole personality is affected.

Our trouble about recognising sin, however, is that we see it in other people much more readily than we see it in ourselves. Perhaps that is why some Christians have concentrated on condemning the sins of the flesh which they see in others and have been blind to the sins of the spirit of which they can be guilty themselves. The devil can be as actively at work within a Christian congregation as he is in a public-house or a brothel.

There can be the pride which is puffed up by personal achievement (and this applies as much to the clergy as to any others) or which shows itself in an exclusive attitude to other churches. There can be the smug respectability which covers a selfishness as hard as rock. There can be the cowardice which refuses to face up to hard issues or to take a stand against open wrong, because of expediency. There can be the indecision which keeps people from committing themselves to some bold or generous course of action. There can be the bland indifference to the needs of others, the careless lack of concern which stems from a preoccupation with one's own comfort and ease. There can be the urge for power in one's own small sphere. The range of sin is infinitely wide. Its attacks are subtly insidious, not least because they are made when we can be most sure of our own goodness.

This is the sin from which Jesus came to save us. Perhaps we can begin to realise that we are involved in His coming only when we see the nature of the sin which nailed Him to the Cross.

The people who crucified Jesus were not gangsters or criminals. Many of them were eminently respectable citizens. The pride of the Pharisees made them bitterly resentful of His claims, as also of the truth which He spoke. That is why they spread gossip and slander about Him, and raked up false witnesses to tell lies about Him at His trial. The Sadducees sank their traditional differences with the Pharisees because they saw in Jesus a threat to their own power and to the profits they made from their black-marketeering in the Temple. It was indecision that led Pilate to hand over to His death a man whom he knew to be innocent. It was the cowardice of the disciples (and who are we to blame them?) which left the Son of God to die alone. It was the essential indifference of the crowds who had hailed Him as King on Palm Sunday which allowed them to be swayed to howl for His crucifixion five days later. In fact the sin that was responsible for the death of Jesus is the sin of which we can be guilty in our own lives every day.

At the bar of history it was not Jesus who was judged when He stood in the court of the high priest and again before

Pilate. It was He who condemned the judges, and it is the Cross which condemns us all. When our pride and disobedience to God break out in the ways of which we have been thinking (and in many other ways too), we are putting Him on the Cross again, and keeping Him there. In John Masefield's poem *The Everlasting Mercy* the Quaker girl says to Saul Kane:

> *"Saul Kane," she said, "when next you drink,*
> *Do me the gentleness to think*
> *That every drop of drink accursed*
> *Makes Christ within you die of thirst,*
> *That every dirty word you say*
> *Is one more flint upon His way,*
> *Another thorn about His head,*
> *Another mock by where He tread,*
> *Another nail, another cross.*
> *All that you are is that Christ's loss."*

That is equally true of the unjust criticism of others which can wound and hurt and destroy. It is true of the bitter envy which can wreck personal relationships, bring to ruin old friendships, corrupt and render useless even the good that men try to do. It is true of the competition which seeks to go one better than one's neighbour, the anger that can flare up in a devastating burst, the hate that mingles with love and drives it away. All this is the work of the devil. It is estrangement from God. It is why Jesus died.

We have, then, to diagnose our sin in the light of the Cross. If we do so, we can find the remedy there also. The Cross shows us what human sin does to Jesus, and at the same time it shows us what God does for us in love. Jesus did not die in order to satisfy an angry God by bearing the punishment which God was determined to exact for man's sin. His death was not a ransom to the devil or a sacrifice whose repetition by a priest assures us of our salvation. Jesus died because "God was in Christ reconciling the world to Himself." He died to show us that the love of God goes to the uttermost in order to bridge the gulf of our estrangement from Him, to restore the relationship we have broken.

We can begin to understand what it means to be "saved" only when we think in terms of personal relationship. The power of evil finds its opportunity in our natural self-centredness. We can be blind to this until we realise that the unhappiness and frustration we experience are due to the breaking of our relationship with God and with other people. For Christian men and women the Cross is the shocking sign of what their sin can do. This means penitence for them, and it also means forgiveness. They come to themselves, as the Prodigal did, and realise that if they are to be made whole they must accept this offer of God's love and turn to Him again. *The Everlasting Mercy* expresses this well when Saul Kane says:

> *I did not think, I did not strive,*
> *The deep peace burnt my me alive;*
> *The bolted door had broken in,*
> *I knew that I had done with sin.*
> *I knew that Christ had given me birth*
> *To brother all the souls on earth.*

This is the heart of the Christian experience; and it is simply a fact that anyone who has glimpsed the reality of God's love in the Cross of Christ knows that he is in touch with a power stronger than the power of evil. It is not that he is immune from its attacks. They will assail him to his dying day. But he knows that love is ultimate reality and that evil is despair and desolation. When pride and selfishness corrupt personal relationships he therefore knows what he must do. He must allow love to have its way with him, for only so will he be able to co-operate with God's purpose for him as an individual. Only so can he find wholeness and integrity.

He will be mistaken, however, if he thinks that he can find this wholeness by himself. The idea of salvation can become a selfish thing if it is separated from the fellowship of the Christian community. It can be selfish if it is concerned only with men's souls and pays no attention to their material and social welfare. It can be selfish if it says that anyone who cannot repeat the orthodox evangelical phrases is not a true Christian. That is why the Church is the means by which individuals can find their wholeness. It is the field in which Christ has chosen to be at work. It is the Body through which His influence can spread into the world. For that reason it can never fulfil its function if it is allowed to become an enclosed society concerned only with keeping the wheels of its organisation turning. It must be a missionary Church, seeking to draw all men into its fellowship, going out in love to restore the harmony which has been broken by sin. It must see the urgency of the battle with the active, personal power of evil.

There is a prayer of St. Francis of Assisi which gives us a picture of the spirit in which we have to fight this battle. It says:

> *Lord, make us instruments of Thy peace.*
> *Where there is hatred, let us sow love;*
> *Where there is injury, pardon;*
> *Where there is discord, union;*
> *Where there is doubt, faith;*
> *Where there is despair, hope;*
> *Where there is darkness, light;*
> *Where there is sadness, joy;*
> *for Thy mercy and for Thy truth's sake.*

This is the power of love at work against the power of evil. We may never be able to answer fully the question of why evil should exist. We can only glimpse the outlines of God's plan for the world, believing that the struggle in which man is involved bears some relation to a splendid, loving purpose which He is working out. The question which really matters is whose side we are on in the battle. If we are in any real sense coping with life, we shall not be merely on the defensive, rocked back on our heels, resigned, submissive and ineffective.

Rather shall we take the field in the spirit of St. Paul's stirring words:

"Finally, then, find your strength in the Lord, in His mighty power. Put on all the armour which God provides, so that you may be able to stand firm against the devices of the devil. For our fight is not against human foes, but against cosmic powers, against the authorities and potentates of this dark world, against the superhuman forces of evil in the heavens. Therefore, take up God's armour; then you will be able to stand your ground when things are at their worst, to complete every task and still to stand."

9

TESTING OF FAITH

ALONG with the problem of evil we have to face the problem of suffering. Once I stood by the bed of quite a young woman who was dying of cancer. She knew what was wrong with her and that she would not live. She was not afraid of death. She bore her pain with uncomplaining courage. The question she asked me was, "Why should this have happened to me at this time?"

It was a hard question to answer. Life had been difficult for her. Her husband had been on the verge of disaster, and she had stood by him with the greatest loyalty. She had salved the wreckage, kept the family together, and seen the children growing up happily. Now, just when it seemed that better times were coming and when the home needed her all the more, she was dying. Her distress was not for herself but for the future of those she loved. "What," she asked, "have I done to deserve this?"

Part of the answer, of course, was to make her realise that her suffering was not in any sense a punishment from God. God takes no delight in the sufferings of His children. He is not an angry potentate who exacts retribution in this way. We can bring punishment upon ourselves by our wrongdoing, but this is not God's will. At least I could assure her of this, and remind her of all the blessings which we take for granted, and which we have done nothing to deserve. I could also have told her of the various theories about the meaning of suffering but that would have been of little use. In the urgency of the situation—and it is one which a minister often has to face— I could only pray with her, ask for God's peace upon her, and tell her that Christ stood beside her in her pain and distress.

There is a place for academic speculation about suffering. We need the writings of the theologians and philosophers to show us possible answers. In my work, however, I have to visit many people who are suffering in one way or another. I find there is a vast difference between viewing suffering as a speculative problem and actually being involved in it. On the theoretical level, suffering can remain a baffling puzzle, however able the arguments for or against belief in God may be. It is when one is involved in suffering, even if only to the extent of trying to help the person who suffers, that a clue to its meaning can be found.

No one wants to suffer. Most of us are afraid of illness. We fear the discomfort and the pain it may entail; we are anxious lest it may leave us disabled or incapacitated for our work. We are frightened of being a liability to ourselves or others. Our imaginations get to work and we picture a dismal future, should we have to suffer in some such way. We are disinclined to believe that an experience of this kind could bring us any good at all.

No one can pretend that illness is something to be welcomed. Yet as I go round week by week visiting people who are ill in hospital or at home, I find that my belief in God is strengthened rather than weakened, and that this is often the experience of the patients themselves.

I know the risk of idealizing or sentimentalizing the impression made on people by the care and treatment they receive in hospital. Uncomplaining sanctity is not a universal characteristic of those who occupy the beds, nor are patience and perfection to be found in all doctors and nurses. It is true, nevertheless, that people can find, through being in hospital, something which they had never foreseen. They fear the pain and the gloomy prospects. They find, in contrast, careful attention, skill and tenderness. They see others, much worse than themselves, setting them an example. They discover that even the toughest characters have a warm human sympathy and readiness to help. Their illness and suffering have opened their eyes to a new depth in human experience and in life itself.

The point is that the very things we dread can be those which form a richer pattern in our lives. When the test comes, we are not likely to turn to the books which give us calm, detached and lucidly intellectual expositions of the problem of suffering, however admirable and useful they may be. We are frightened human beings looking for strength and guidance. We are on the spot ourselves, being tried as to whether or not our theoretical belief is valid in practice. This is where we need a deep-rooted faith which will begin to function. This, in fact, is where we have to take Jesus at His word.

Jesus never said that we should escape suffering if we followed Him, but He did say that He would help us to overcome it. The Cross of Jesus is central in Christianity. Theoretically it is perplexing, puzzling and agonizing. But if we are involved in suffering we find that this is where the Cross means something vital, and Christianity makes a difference. One can see this working not only in the acceptance of illness but also in the healing process. Faith does help recovery on the part of the patient, just as it can be active in the attitude of a nurse or a doctor who is a Christian.

This, then, is part of the answer I have found. In theory the problem of suffering remains. In practice one can find the truth of the words of Jesus, "In the world you will have trouble. But courage! The victory is mine; I have conquered the world."

It is one thing, however, to speak of illness successfully cured. It is another thing to face suffering which continues and which seems unlikely to be relieved. This is where tragedy and heartbreak challenge us. As a parish minister I have been brought in touch with many such cases. I can only say that the great majority of them have held to the Faith and inspired others by their courage.

I think, for example, of a woman who was bed-ridden for

ten years with multiple sclerosis. She was a university graduate who had done interesting and worthwhile work in her short career. She had to give this up and accept the prospect of a long and lingering illness. It would have been only too easy to complain and be bitter. In all the years I knew her I never heard her do so. She kept alive her interest in other people and in all that was going on. Her sick-room was never a gloomy place, no matter how weak she was. After she died, her Bible was found to be marked at Romans 8: 17: "We are God's heirs and Christ's fellow-heirs, if we share his sufferings now in order to share his splendour hereafter." Somehow, she had been able to offer her suffering to God and to know the companionship of Christ.

Perhaps this is the essential difference made by the Christian Faith. Courage is not a Christian monopoly. Unbelievers can show fine examples of fortitude in the face of suffering. There is a certain nobility in W. E. Henley's lines, which express the view of an agnostic:

> Out of the night that covers me,
> Black as the Pit from pole to pole,
> I thank whatever gods may be
> For my unconquerable soul.
>
> In the fell clutch of circumstance,
> I have not winced nor cried aloud:
> Under the bludgeonings of chance
> My head is bloody, but unbowed.

This is man standing on his own against what he sees as a meaningless universe, shaking his fist at it, defying the worst that it may do to him. I may have a certain admiration for such an attitude but I cannot share it. It is too proud. It can so easily become embittered. It rejects the idea of any overruling purpose. If I am a Christian I know that I cannot "go it alone" in my own strength. Instead of clinging to the shreds of my pride I have to be dependent on God. Even if the meaning seems shrouded in uncertainty I know that I must go on seeking it. Above all I must believe that what seems to be evil can be turned to good.

I can only testify that I have seen this happening, and that I believe the Christian Faith to be responsible for it. Another woman whom I know had a devastating experience. She was a scientist with high qualifications, and there was every prospect that she would go steadily ahead in her profession. Then, literally out of the blue, the blow fell.

Her great interest, apart from her work, was climbing. One winter day, when she was on a Highland mountain, an avalanche swept down upon her and her companion as they were climbing roped together. Her friend was comparatively unscathed, but she was paralysed from the waist down.

All the elements of undeserved suffering were there. There seemed to be no meaning in what had happened. The accident was not her fault. She was a good and careful climber, and she and her friend were taking all reasonable precautions. Why such suffering, if God is in His heaven?

One can argue that suffering is a trial and a test of faith, that it brings out reserves of human character, that it can enrich and deepen the personality of the sufferer. All this may indeed be true, but when suffering comes it cannot be viewed in a detached and theoretical way. Suffering can be ugly, cruel and humiliating. Does one therefore reject belief in God? On the contrary, this is where one finds the reality of a Faith at whose heart there is a Cross which was ugly, cruel and humiliating. Indeed it is precisely through contact with suffering that one can find how the Cross ceases to be the decorative symbol of a pious respectability, and stands out in its stark reality as a clue to the meaning of existence, as an answer to the problem of suffering, as a light in the thickest darkness. It is too easy to admire paintings of the Crucifixion without realising what it meant for the Man who was crucified. The hymns which are sung about the Cross can be associated more readily with comfortable churches than with the spasms of a tortured and naked body. It is perhaps in the experience of suffering that people can come closest to the Christ who died on the Cross.

Certainly this woman had more than enough to endure. There were the pain and discomfort which continued for months. There was the loss of bodily movement and all the indignity it involved. There was the searing anxiety about the future. All this she bore with grit, and determination to get back eventually to her work, despite the fact that she had been told that she would never walk again. There were, however, two things which I noticed in her reaction to the catastrophe, and they seemed to me to be of fundamental importance.

The first was that from the beginning her attitude was positive. She could have allowed herself to become bitter and hopeless. Instead she began to climb up painfully, as it were inch by inch, from the bottom of the hill. This was not only an effort towards recovery on the physical level. It was also a mental and spiritual readjustment and development.

Whether one accepts the Christian Faith or not, there is no doubt that it is better to be positive than despairing. Whether one can solve the problem of suffering intellectually or not, one can see which is the more effective attitude towards it. In this context it is crucial to remember that Jesus hated the thought of having to die on the Cross, and prayed that He might be spared it. None the less His attitude was positive. His suffering was not imposed upon Him but was freely undertaken, when He believed it to be God's will, as a necessary part of His work and mission.

The second thing I noticed was contained in something she said to me when I saw her in hospital. We had been speaking about all that her paralysis had meant in frustration and re-adjustment, and she said quite simply, "I feel that there is a meaning in all this and that my job is to find it." Since then she has justified her words. She cannot walk, but she is back at her work. With the help of various appliances, she can live alone in her house, drive herself to her work and do her full daily stint. She flew to Australia for the Paraplegic Empire Games, and came back with a gold and a bronze medal. She is finding more of the meaning in what has happened.

If we can face suffering like this we are, perhaps, as near as we can be to coping with it. There are times when people find it almost impossible to see any sense or reason in the tragic things which happen. It is then that they can remember the cry of Jesus on the Cross, "My God, my God, why hast Thou forsaken me?" I do not think that Jesus had ceased to believe in God when He said that, but I do think that momentarily He had lost the sense of purpose in what was happening, and it all seemed meaningless futility.

We must also set against this cry of dereliction His other words from the Cross, "Father, into Thy hands I commit my spirit." Once more He trusted God's purpose. We know that He was right in doing so; but what we need also to realise is that when we are up against it He is still right and that there is a meaning to be found. If the Cross is truly central in our faith, and if we turn to it in our need, I am confident that the worst that can happen will not destroy us.

When I think of all the suffering in the world I am only too conscious of the inadequacy of anything that I can say in an attempt to explain it. I only know that I have found glimmerings of the truth, mostly shown to me by others. I know that when people hold on to the belief that there is a purpose, wider than they can see, working out in their lives, they will never give in. I also like to believe that whether they are professing Christians or not, their experience is bringing them very close to the Jesus who suffered on the Cross and rose again in victory over the worst that life could do to Him. I think that they can be finding out more about God all the time, through the help which others give them, through the way in which even the most unlikely people stand by them in their need, and through the recovery of a faith and insight which they thought they had lost.

This was brought home to me when I received a letter, after

a *Coping with Life* broadcast, from a man whom I had not seen for thirty years. He and I had been at school together, but afterwards our paths had separated, and I had no idea of where he was or what he was doing until his letter arrived.

Life had dealt hardly with him. He had done well in his profession and had served right through the war on several fronts, having been mentioned in dispatches. Peace had brought a series of disasters and misfortunes—seven major operations, high blood pressure and several bouts of pneumonia. After ten years of happy marriage his wife had died of cancer and his health had broken down so completely that he had to leave Scotland for premature retirement in the south of England. He poured all this out to me in his letter, which had been prompted by the sight of a former schoolmate talking on television about the Christian Faith. "I am not in a sense a religious man," he wrote, "but I feel better after having heard one of your talks." And again, "I rather feel sometimes that life has been unjust and unkind to me and my faith wavers and flickers."

I wrote back to him at once, but as I wrote in longhand I kept no copy of my letter and I cannot remember exactly what I said. I only know that I felt it was inadequate to his need, and I doubted if it would do any good. So indeed it seemed, for the days passed and I heard no more.

Then, nine months later, he wrote again, "You will be surprised to hear from me, but I feel the need of some guidance, sympathy and prayer, in all of which you may be able to help me." He went on to say that he had gone to hospital for another operation which had been followed by an alarming kind of paralysis. Although he had recovered from this, it had left him shaken and all the more depressed.

"You told me," he wrote, "not to lose faith, but I feel at a time like this mine is more than strained. I really feel rather afraid, and I don't like the feeling one little bit. It must seem stupid to you my writing to you after all these years, but I shall be most pleased to receive any advice you have to give.

Please do offer up a prayer on my behalf, and I trust that I will be with you in spirit as you do so."

Again I saw the limitations of long-range correspondence, and it became clear to me that he needed Christian fellowship. I told him that we should pray for him in our church at our weekly service of intercession for the sick, but that he must think about getting in touch with a local church. I confess I wondered if he would think this fatuous.

A month later his reply came, and it was obvious that he was still a prickly Scot. He wrote, "I had a visit in hospital from the Church of England curate, and told him off for their refusal to give Holy Communion to any except their 'ain folk'. I also listened in to a broadcast Communion Service and was not impressed one little bit."

I felt the barriers were building up. Here was a man needing spiritual help, needing in fact the full sacramental worship of the Church. What did "validity" of orders and apostolic succession mean to him in his distress? He was separated from his own Communion and the only congregation within reasonable distance of him belonged to the Church of England. I was still determined, if possible, to persuade him to link up with the Church again, and said so in my reply, although I knew that there might be some difficulty about admitting him to the Sacrament.

A situation like this pinpoints the urgency of the present welcome movement towards unity between the Churches. We need to remember that Jesus came to help human beings in distress. We are too ready to use His name to justify our prejudices and to bolster up our claims to be historically respectable or ecclesiastically correct. A great many of the obstacles which churchmen discover in the path to unity are quite incomprehensible to average people. It is too easy to say that in the churches we are bound by our rules. If our rules keep us from fulfilling the real function of the Church, it is time we thought hard about changing them.

At the beginning of the following year, he wrote, "I had a

very quiet but quite happy Christmas here, and on Christmas Day went to the Church of England, incense and all! Communion was celebrated, but I just did not go forward." I could picture the scene clearly—a stranger, a Scot, a Presbyterian, wanting something badly, but feeling himself an outsider, with his racial hackles rising at the sight of what savoured of meaningless ritual in his nostrils. He was, however, beginning to thaw. "The vicar," he said, "preached a good sermon, and the service was quite interesting." Then he told me the vicar's name, and I felt that Providence had begun to take a hand.

My mind went back to a Remembrance Day service in the 'thirties in Govan Old Parish Church where I was an assistant minister. Several local clergy were combining in the service, among them a Scottish Episcopalian. I had a vivid memory of him in his white surplice, striding down the chancel to read the lesson at the lectern. The opening words echoed the question in the minds of the Govan congregation (perhaps a little suspicious of strangers in their midst) as the Episcopalian read in ringing tones, "What are these which are arrayed in white robes? and whence came they?"

This was the same man whose church my friend had attended, and I felt sure that he would be able to help. I could see that there was now a real opportunity and that the wanderer was on his way home, when he wrote, "I have definitely made up my mind to attend church regularly, as I feel deeply the Good Lord must have been with me during the past six months, and in this way only, as far as I can see, can I give thanks."

After this the letters began to come thick and fast. The local church was in action, the vicar was on the job and the bishop of the diocese was to be consulted. My friend was beginning to find the reality of fellowship. "I had reached the stage," his letter said, "of envying people who attended church regularly, and convinced myself I was very definitely missing something."

From this stage a new note emerged in his letters. There was no more questioning, no trace of bitterness, but instead an acceptance of what life had brought and a serenity which had replaced his previous frustration. It was no accident that this went along with his new practice of going to church every Sunday, and of dropping in to the church for a few minutes nearly every day to say a prayer.

He had also rediscovered the Bible, particularly through J. B. Phillips's translation of the New Testament, and he wrote, "Life has taken a turn for the better, and I feel better mentally and physically for it. In my ignorance and stupidity I had given the Church up as 'no good'. Well, we live, suffer and learn. My only complaint is why some of us have to suffer so much in contrast with others." In reply I quoted to him the words of Psalm 73 : v. 16, "When I thought to know this, it was too painful for me, until I went into the sanctuary of God", urging him to continue in the Church at all costs.

A month later, just before Palm Sunday, he wrote to say that he didn't know what I would think, but he had decided to accept the bishop's invitation to be confirmed in the Church of England. He felt, I imagine, that I might be annoyed at a Scottish Presbyterian going over to the Anglicans. So far from that, it gave me great joy to read in his letter that he enjoyed his worship, and that he had come to the point where he realised that it was no good being sorry for himself and expecting the Almighty to do everything to help him, instead of going to His House and seeking Him through prayer.

When next he wrote, the experience of his confirmation was fresh in his mind, and he spoke of all it had meant to him, "Through you all, in spite of all the adversities I have had since the war, my faith, once really shattered, has risen again." I asked him if sometime I might tell others about his spiritual pilgrimage, and he replied, "If any of my problems are of help, certainly please use them; but there must be many worse off than myself."

I had two more letters, in which he told me that he had to go into hospital for another operation. He had no word of complaint, and wrote with great courage and cheerfulness, saying in the final paragraph of his last letter, "I believe one hands over one's life to the Almighty and the capable and gifted hands of the surgeon." He knew that we were still praying for him at our little service every Sunday evening in our church.

A fortnight later I was visiting Brathay Hall on Lake Windermere, which is a training centre for lads, run on "Outward Bound" lines. I was there, strangely enough, because the Warden had asked me to give a talk after having seen the same television programme which had first led my friend to write to me. I was looking over my notes when the telephone bell rang. The call was for me, and it was to tell me that my friend had died, quite suddenly, after having come safely through the operation.

It was a wonderful June evening, and as I looked over the still waters of the lake I thought of the words of Mr. Valiant-for-Truth as he came to the river of death, with its deep-running waters,

" 'My sword I give to him that will succeed me in my pilgrimage, and my courage and skill to him that can get it. My marks and my scars I carry with me, to be a witness that I have fought His battles, who now will be my rewarder.' When the day that he must go hence was come, many accompanied him to the riverside, into which as he went he said, 'Death, where is thy sting?' And as he went down deeper, he said, 'Grave, where is thy victory?' So he passed over, and all the trumpets sounded for him on the other side."

We may never be able fully to solve the problem of suffering. Perhaps this matters less than that we should find a means of coping with it. The Cross of Jesus shows us that He suffers with us. His Resurrection assures us that the victory can be won and that God's purpose is not limited to this world. Our faith can still be "the victory that defeats the world".

GRIT FOR THE ROAD

ALTHOUGH Christianity is realistic in its view of sin and suffering, it is not gloomy. It is true that the impression can be given that Christians spend their time in condemning sin and being resigned to suffering in the hope that they will find their reward and their release in heaven. Here is a verse from a hymn which could hardly be said to convey the spirit of gaiety:

> *We smite the breast, we weep in vain,*
> *In vain for sins we mourn,*
> *Unless with penitential pain*
> *The smitten soul be torn.*

One could, of course, say in defence that these words contain a germ of truth, and that they are no more gloomy than much of the lovesick wailing which can be heard on "Juke Box Jury". They fail, however, to express the essential gladness of faith. In the same way a wrong impression of eternal life can be given by the verse:

> *Brief life is here our portion,*
> *Brief sorrow, short-lived care;*
> *The life that knows no ending,*
> *The tearless life is there.*

Taken literally, this bids us put up with life on earth as a dismal prelude to life hereafter. This is not what Jesus taught about eternal life. For Him it was to be found in the present, in the here and now. Life is compact of joy and sorrow, of laughter and tears, but for those who follow Him the note of gladness should predominate. Our conviction must be that at the heart of things there are goodness and love. It is in the Book of Job, with all its emphasis on sin and suffering, that we hear the trumpet call to believe in the purpose of a creation, "When the morning stars sang together, and all the sons of God shouted for joy."

I have a letter which I cherish, because it seems to me to express the essence of this attitude in simple and homely terms. It came from an old-age pensioner. She lives in a single room which is always clean and bright. She has no relatives. She is far from well, and she has constant pain. She is also one of the most cheerful and happy people I know. Her letter read,

"Dear Friend,
I hope that I will see you soon. I had a visit from your Assistant. We had a good laugh and a lovely prayer.
Your friend,
Bella."

"A good laugh and a lovely prayer." That seems to me to be an admirable conjunction. As W. B. Yeats has written,

For the good are always the merry,
Save by an evil chance.

In our moments of depression this is something to remember. We have no Scriptural warrant for spreading about us an atmosphere of gloom.

When my father was in India, part of his work was to supervise two leper asylums. In those days the treatment of leprosy was not as far advanced as it is now. I have photographs which show some of these lepers with their disfigured faces and their maimed limbs. Another letter which I treasure came from them, sending their good wishes at my graduation. That they wrote at all was due to the work my father had done with them. A friend said of him after his death, "I was never so proud of him as when I saw him among the lepers —those children of sorrow—winning them all to laugh along with him."

This is no superficial joviality. It is not a question of going about with a fixed and toothy grin. Rather is it akin to the words of an old Scottish Covenanter, "Werena' my he'rt licht, I wad dee." One does not associate gaiety with those stern preachers of "The Killing Time" in Scotland. Yet it was one of them, with the unpromising name of Ephraim McBriar, who said as he lay waiting for his execution, "I am not so cumbered about dying as I have often been about preaching a sermon." Over two centuries later, Scott of the Antarctic wrote of his companions in the tent where they were to die, "It would do your heart good to be in our tent and to hear our songs and the cheery conversation. We have decided to die naturally in the track. We could have got through if we had neglected our sick."

Such a spirit is a constant inspiration and challenge, not least when we feel the black dog of care upon our backs. If ever I am jaded and depressed there is one certain cure. It is to get out among other people, visit them in their homes, share their interests and their happiness, try to stand beside them in their trouble and their sorrow. So often one finds that others have so much more to endure, and yet contrive to keep cheerful. Depression feeds itself all the more when it remains alone. It is when we forget ourselves that we begin to find gladness again.

An old Indian scripture says, "Were there no spirit of joy in the universe, who could live and breathe in this world of life?" St. Augustine gave a Christian expression to the same thought when he wrote, "The Holy Spirit is a glad spirit." This stems from the teaching and Person of Jesus Himself. To be sure He is "A man of sorrows and acquainted with grief", but no one can think of Him as a gloomy ascetic. He came that men might have life and have it more abundantly.

He showed what this life was like in His relationship with all kinds of people. He enjoyed their friendship. He was invited to their weddings and to supper in their homes. It was the staid and "unco' guid" Pharisees who gossiped about Him as a glutton and wine-bibber. He loved nature and He loved children. Life for Him was a gift from God which was to be used to the full. A sinner was someone who had "missed the mark", the lost sheep to be brought back with rejoicing, the prodigal to be welcomed with music and dancing. We cannot forget that "He set His face resolutely towards Jerusalem" to meet His death. Yet on the night of His agony, He said to His disciples, "I have spoken thus to you, so that my joy may be in you, and your joy complete."

It was on the same night that He gave us the Sacrament of His Body and His Blood. In Scotland there has been a tendency to turn this Sacrament into a sad memorial of His death, and to forget that it is a glad Communion with the living Lord. The Cross was followed by and cannot be separated from the Resurrection. Jesus died to rise again. He died that we might live. Bread is the symbol of the bread we earn by our daily work. As the Bread is broken we remember that His Body was broken on the Cross so that we might be led to glorify God in the work we do. Wine is the symbol of the richness and beauty of life. As the Wine is poured we remember that His Blood was shed in order that men might not throw loveliness into the gutter, but learn to praise God in the enjoyment of life. Each time we make our Communion we can offer to God every part of our lives. Religion is not confined to stated services and ceremonial occasions. It covers the whole of life. It should be in everything that we do. "The Holy Spirit is a glad spirit."

By the same token, there is no happiness to be found in evil. It is a dismal business. As G. K. Chesterton said:

> *Now who that runs can read it,*
> *The riddle that I write,*

Of why this poor old sinner
Should sin without delight—
But I, I cannot read it
(Although I run and run),
Of them that do not have the faith,
And will not have the fun.

It is a pity that more Christians have not realised the strength of wit and humour as weapons in their armoury. They are most certainly gifts of God. They should be used in His cause, instead of being left to the cynics and the exponents of "sick" humour. It has been part of my ministerial duty to attend various public dinners. At some of them I have been bored to tears, not least by the dreary convention which causes middle-aged business men to deliver themselves of the kind of smut which one had associated with prurient adolescence. Such behaviour is less wicked than sadly silly and immature. It needs both the whip of scorn to subdue it and the salt of wit to dispel it. I was glad to hear J. B. Morton ("Beachcomber" of the *Daily Express*) say in a television interview that he held certain beliefs very strongly, and that he used his column to ridicule anything which sought to degrade the values he cherished. There is nothing the devil hates so much as being laughed at, and it is high time that the myth was exploded which pretends that loose living is the path to gaiety and happiness.

This myth has been sedulously fostered by a good deal of modern sophisticated writing. One notices it both in the "intellectual" weeklies, and in the "quality" Sunday newspapers. One gets the impression that the Ward case and the Profumo affair shook the complacency of those who had so strenuously ridiculed what they dubbed as "Puritanism". For that reason they have continued to play down as harmless what the majority of people in this country still regard as a complete denial of mature and wholesome living.

These are defensive tactics, and they should be met with a determined attack by Christian public opinion. It is so ridiculous to maintain that drugs, alcohol, night-clubs and strip-tease shows are the summit of enjoyment for twentieth-century people, or that a man is happy only when he can keep both a mistress and a wife. Where are we to find delight in living? Certainly not through the kerb-crawling cars of our city streets, nor through the so-called pleasures of excessive drinking. I have seen enough of alcoholism to know that it is not a pretty thing. I am not a strict teetotaller, but if anyone tells me that the full life is to be seen in the glazed eye, the staggering step, the crude guffaw or the careless hand on the steering wheel, I laugh at the proposition. This is the poor old sinner who sins without delight. More often than not he is trying to escape from a life in which he has found no joy. He needs to be pitied and helped. It is those who would try to defend his plight as being an example of the right of the individual to self-expression who need to be ridiculed.

At the same time, one would have to admit that Christians themselves are not always examples of joyous living. It was said of St. Francis Xavier by one of his fellow-missionaries that whenever any brother was down-hearted he would go and look at Francis's face, and straightway his heart was warmed and cheered. Not many of us are able to keep such a standard consistently. Sometimes, in the words of Norman MacLeod's hymn, our road through life is "rough and dreary" and "its end far out of sight". We feel that we ought to "foot it bravely", but the plain truth is that we have no joy in what we are doing, our steps are heavy and our hearts are leaden.

At least we can remember that this is an experience which the greatest saints have known. "The dark night of the soul" may come upon us. We must endure it, but we can also come through it. Baron von Hügel, in a letter to his niece who had spoken of passing through such a time, gave her a picture of how to cope with it. He told her to imagine that she was climbing a mountain, and this might mean that

she was enveloped in mist for days on end, unable to see a
foot before her. Experienced mountaineers do not rush their
ascent. They have a quiet, regular, short step. When such a
mountaineer finds the thick mists coming down, he does
not lose his head or give up the climb. He halts and camps
under some slight cover, eating his rations, quietly smoking
his pipe, and moving on only when the mist has cleared
away. In the same way, said von Hügel, she would have to
accept the dark times without losing faith, and find that they
could be fruitful.

To change the picture, one can think of what the Letter to
the Hebrews says about the Christian life as a race. It is no
short sprint, but rather a long relay race in which the torch
has been handed on to us by those who have gone before.
"And what of ourselves?" says the writer. "With all these
witnesses to faith around us like a cloud, we must throw off
every encumbrance, every sin to which we cling, and run
with resolution the race for which we are entered, our eyes
fixed on Jesus, on whom faith depends from start to finish."
Life is not a joy-ride. It is a race to be run with resolution.
As old Giles Hoggett said to Mr. Crawley in Trollope's
Last Chronicles of Barset, "It's dogged as does it. It ain't
thinking about it."

Perhaps we feel the strain of the race most in the middle
years of life. The first flush of youth has gone. We can no
longer "mount up with wings as eagles". The quieter days of
retirement are still in the distance, when we "can walk and
not faint". The testing time of the race comes when we are
in the middle of it. This is when, in the words of Isaiah, we
have to "run and not be weary". It is the time when people
either begin to achieve their aims or begin to crack up. It is
the time when mind and heart should have matured with
experience, but when the body feels the strain. It is the time
for great things to be done, and also for physical and nervous
breakdowns. It is when we begin to get our second wind, or
when we flag and fall behind in the race.

Here is a mother strained to the utmost in dealing with the problems of a growing family. There is a man who has spent his energy in service and is beginning to "tire of doing good". They need staying power. Even when they feel that they can go no farther they have to set their teeth and carry on. This need be no grim or joyless effort, as long as a sense of purpose is retained. The race must be run with resolution, but it can also be run with zest.

It was with this in mind that I once gave a talk in the *Coping with Life* series on "The Road *from* the Isles". It was on the theme of returning from holidays to everyday living. The title was due to our family custom of going on holiday to the West Highlands of Scotland along "The Road to the Isles" made famous by Kenneth MacLeod's lilting song,

> *Sure by Tummel and Loch Rannoch and Lochaber I will go,*
> *By heather tracks with heaven in their wiles.*

This was the road we travelled year after year. It was always a joy to leave the city behind and to set out for a countryside which (at least for a Scot) is unequalled in beauty by any part of the world. One drank in the matchless combination of mountains and lochs, of sky and sea, of creaming waves and dazzling white sands from which one could look out to the Coolins of Skye and the blue islands of the west. One revelled in the peace and quiet of the first evening stroll down to a little bay where the still waters (granted that the weather was good) reflected the red and gold of a glorious sunset. Convention and artificiality were left behind. Whether it rained or not (and it can rain in the West Highlands), one knew that there would be time to read, to walk, to talk, to enjoy the company of family and friends, to find both recreation and re-creation. On the first night of the holidays it seemed a long time before one had to take up the race again.

Yet the days passed all too quickly and it was no time before one was on "The Road *from* the Isles". In a flash the holiday had gone, and it was back to the grindstone, back to urban civilisation (so-called), back to the threat of occupational diseases—nervous tension, duodenal ulcer or coronary thrombosis. The old problems loomed ahead, with the added menace of new ones as yet unknown.

There was, however, a signpost which could be seen on the road which we travelled, and which had a message of encouragement. It stood a little to the side of the road. Beside it was a pile of small stones mixed with sand, and it read simply, "Grit for Roads". These Highland roads are tricky and narrow. At steep hills and hairpin bends grit is needed for the surface when it becomes slippery with rain or dangerous with ice. The road may be difficult, but if there is "Grit for the Road" the journey can still be a grand one, full of interest and joy.

None of us is likely to find his or her road through life easy or free from snags and difficulties. This does not keep it from being packed with richness and variety. To find this, however, "Grit for the Road" is needed, in the sense of faith and determination to carry on. Hills are there to be climbed, snags to be overcome; and our difficulties can be the opportunities which we are given to show what our faith really means. "Grit for the Road" was a simple thought, but it meant something to me.

It was encouraging to find that it also meant something to other people. Two years after I had used the illustration I was on holiday in another part of the West Highlands and met a lady who told me what it had meant to her. She had heard the talk soon after she had returned from a wonderful holiday with her husband and small daughter on a western island. Six days before this she had been told by the family doctor that her husband—who had seemed perfectly well on holiday —would only have a few months to live. She was completely stunned. As she told me, she felt that nothing would ever be right again.

On the Sunday night she was sitting at her husband's feet, watching "Meeting Point". In her own words to me, she felt something speak directly to her husband and herself. She knew that in the testing time ahead she must remember "Grit for the Road", and she found that strength was given to her to face everything.

This feeling continued through the whole illness. She and her husband had a wonderfully happy winter, in spite of the fact that he was in much pain. The specialist who treated him told her that he had never known so brave a patient. As the end came near, she found that she was able to accept the fact that he was going, without despair. He was at peace, the pain was gone; and as she sat by his bedside she felt that God was very near. "Grit for the Road" had made all the difference. Nor was this a passing phase. Three years later I met her again, and she was still running the race with zest and resolution.

I mention her experience not because I take the credit for it. In actual fact, the idea of the illustration was not my own. I had roughed out the script for the talk when I was on holiday at Arisaig. My friend, Ronald Falconer of the BBC, was producing the programme, and he came up to Arisaig to spend a night and to discuss the production. He had taken several photographs on the way for the purpose of visual illustrations, and he had spotted this sign which he suggested I might use. I did so, and this was one of the results. The point is simply that any "preacher of the word" can be an instrument whom God can use, and it seemed that He had done so in this instance.

In God is our sufficiency. It is when we "wait upon Him" (as Isaiah says) that we can "run and not be weary." Again and again I have seen people coming through the most difficult times without losing heart. Had they known before what they would have to face they might have quailed at the prospect. In the event, they won through; and how often they have said to me that they received a strength which they never expected to have, and which came to them from outside themselves.

Another memory I carry with me from my holidays is of the Coolins of Skye. They never looked the same from one day to another. Sometimes they stood sharply etched against the evening sky. Again they were swathed in a golden mist. One morning they could be friendly, with the wind chasing the cloud shadows across their slopes. The next they could be grim and lowering, like a threat of judgment. They were always changing, but they were always the same, as they had been for countless generations. They gave one a feeling of enduring stability.

How much more can we believe that God is always the same. There are times when the clouds seem to blot Him out altogether, but it is not merely in the golden days that we can be sure of Him. He is with us in the storm and the thick darkness. We can be sure of Him when the murk and gloom and vice of the city streets swirl round us. Even when problems and pain, sickness and death advance against us like spectres, God is always there. He has given us the race to run, with resolution and zest. He is with us on the road, and with Him it can become for us the King's Highway along which we journey with joy in our hearts.

THE ROAD AHEAD

IT is all very well, it might be argued, to talk about "Grit for the Road", but what of the future which we face as Christians in the modern world? If we picture the human race as being on a journey, what kind of road lies ahead?

The climate of opinion in which we live reflects what has been called secular optimism. It looks ahead to an age of increasing scientific and technological advance. Man has advanced farther in the last fifty years than in the sum of the preceding centuries. This is the jet-propelled age. It means motor highways, and the Buchanan Report on town-planning. It means space travel. It means man's increasing mastery over nature. There is nothing which he will be unable to achieve.

It all sounds wonderful, and one can understand how secular man sees little relevance, in such a future, for what he may consider to be the antiquated ideas of Christianity. None the less Christians must point out that while man may claim to be master of the natural world, he still remains strangely unable to control his own nature. He may achieve a landing on the moon, but there will still be a multitude of problems on the earth which he has left unsolved. He may cope with all kinds of scientific issues, but he finds it extremely difficult to cope with himself.

Recently I was invited by the Scottish Humanist Conference to take part in a public debate on the motion "That Humanism today is a better basis for purposeful living than Christianity". This seemed to me to epitomise the attitude which I have just been describing, and I went to the debate with some trepidation. In the event I was encouraged and strengthened in my own beliefs. I may not have presented them very adequately, but I was confirmed in my view that Christianity is much more realistic than humanism. My humanist friends, once they had finished condemning the Christian Church, had extraordinarily little that was positive to say about the way in which man must tackle his problems. Their general view was that if we evolved new techniques of treating each other properly, all would be well. They appeared to me to be enveloped in a rosy haze of naïve optimism.

I believed, of course, that they were sincerely concerned about morals and standards of behaviour. Most of the humanists I know strike me as being nice people, and many of them engage in good works. I felt, however, that I had to point out to them that they must realise their share of responsibility for the lowered standards and the moral confusion of the present time. Their representative writers and thinkers had consistently attacked the basis of Christian belief. They had given people the impression that the Bible was discredited and that the Church was the opponent of progress. In consequence they had helped to remove the foundations of morality without replacing them. And I instanced H. G. Wells who, after a lifetime spent in attacking Christianity, in the book written just before his death described humanity as rats leaving the sinking ship of civilisation.

As we look to the road ahead in the second half of the twentieth century I find my mind going back to the words of Jeremiah, "Thus saith the Lord, stand ye in the ways, and see, and ask for the old paths, where is the good way, and walk therein, and ye shall find rest for your souls." If the humanists win the day, I am convinced that things will grow steadily worse. For that reason alone I believe that the Church must go on to the attack. Of course it will be called backward-looking and reactionary; but that does not matter. We have to fight, and fight hard, for what we believe must be preserved.

These words of Jeremiah were not spoken by a backward-looking reactionary who was no longer "with it". Jeremiah was, in fact, much more "with it" than any of his contemporaries. He lived at a time when national morale was low, when people were greedy for material possessions, and were putting a higher value on things than on persons. It was a time when a man's word had ceased to be his bond. Falsehood and broken promises had become too common. Certain smooth characters went about saying, "Peace, peace," when there was no peace. "Not to worry!" one can hear them crying, "Materially we are doing well. Forget the past and look to the brightness of the future. Pay no heed to the gloomy prophecies of those who want to recall days which are gone for ever."

Jeremiah's time was thus not unlike our own. It is plain, however, that he was a true existentialist, in that his concern was with the present in which he lived. He knew that what had given the life of the people reality in the past had been their consciousness of God as the living God for each day and generation. These were the old paths which they had forsaken, and to which he was recalling them.

He wanted them to see that while the conditions of life changed, God did not change. God only showed Himself in a new way in every new age. Once the people had thought that God was to be found localized only in the ark of the covenant. "Away with the idea!" cried Jeremiah, "God is to be found everywhere." Once they had thought that the old covenant of the Ten Commandments given on Mount Sinai was the final word God had to say. "Don't believe it!" said Jeremiah, "The time has come for God to lead you on further, and to write a new covenant in your hearts." This man was no reactionary. He was recalling men to the old paths which contain a message for every new age. Man must learn from the past if he is to cope with life in the present and "greet the unseen with a cheer".

In the West Highlands of Scotland one can still travel along some of the old roads. They are being replaced, of course, but the process is slow, not least because in the West Highlands there seems to be no clear distinction between time and eternity. The day will inevitably come, however, when they are gone for good. When this happens one can only hope that we shall carry with us into the new age the lessons which they taught us. In parable, they apply to the road ahead for us all.

Anyone who has ever travelled along such a road will have found that he has to go slowly. This is no bad thing in the days of motor highways when the scenery tends to become an elongated blur. The old roads are gateways to beauty. There is time to absorb and drink in the delight and refreshment of the natural world. The hills can speak to us and the peace of running water can trickle into our souls. We go slowly enough to enjoy our journey.

In contrast, our modern pace of living gives us too little time to think about the meaning and purpose, let alone the delight of our way through life. There is an old story of a group of simple, primitive animists in South India who went on their first railway journey. They had booked for several stations ahead, but at the first stop they all bundled out on to the platform. When asked why they did so, they replied that their bodies had travelled so fast on the train that they must stop a while in order to let their souls catch up with them.

In his *Memories, Dreams, Reflections,* C. G. Jung underlined the same truth. Writing of the dangers of what we call progress, he said, "It is precisely the loss of connection with the past, our up-rootedness, which has given rise to the 'discontents' of civilisation and to such a flurry and haste that we live more in the future and its chimerical promises of a golden age than in the present with which our evolutionary background has not yet caught up. We rush impetuously into novelty, driven by a mounting sense of insufficiency, dissatisfaction and restlessness. . . . We refuse to recognise that everything better is purchased at the price of something worse; that, for example, the hope of greater freedom is cancelled out by increased enslavement to the state, not to speak of the terrible perils to which the most brilliant discoveries of science expose us. The less we understand of what our fathers and fore-fathers sought, the less we understand ourselves, and thus we help with all our might to rob the individual of his roots and guiding instincts, so that he becomes a particle in the mass, ruled only by what Nietzsche called the spirit of gravity."

Another apparent defect in the old roads is that they are so narrow. When two cars meet, their drivers have to look for a passing place where one can draw in to let the other pass. It is easy to spot a newcomer to such roads by his unwilling-ness to accept their limitations. He has the itch of hurry be-tween his shoulders. He is liable to push on rather rudely until he learns his lesson by going into the ditch. Courtesy is something which has to be learned as a necessary rule of the road in the West Highlands. The narrow way makes us realise that if we are to progress we must love our neighbours as ourselves.

When Jesus said that the way to eternal life was narrow, He did not mean that it was joyless. He was simply telling us that we cannot live unto ourselves. If we are to have abundant life it can only be within the limits set by the law of love for God and for neighbour. When men disregard these limits, they crash, whether it be in a road accident or in some personal disaster. The old paths can teach us that it is in loving God that we learn to love our neighbour, and that through loving our neighbour we find what it means to love God. The humanist error is to think that we can dispense with God and still love our neighbours. We need both rules, and also God's help to keep them.

This was brought home to me one day when I was visiting a hospital ward. I saw a man I knew lying in bed. When I asked him what his illness was, he told me that he had had a coronary thrombosis while playing golf in a monthly medal competition with three others. Incredible as it must seem, his companions had asked a passer-by to go for a doctor, and had left him lying at the side of the fairway while they went on to finish their round. Nor had one of them thought it worth while to visit him in hospital. In comparison with this behaviour, the priest and the Levite on the road from Jerusalem to Jericho seem quite decent types. After all, they had not been introduced to the man who lay wounded on the road.

I told my congregation about this one Sunday, and many of them were inclined to disbelieve me. One lady, however, capped my story with one of her own. She told me of an elderly woman who had a heart attack during a rubber of bridge at a bridge club. When a doctor eventually arrived he found her lying on the floor, covered with a fur coat (a nice touch) while the other ladies played three-handed bridge (known appropriately as cut-throat) to complete the rubber.

These are factual examples of what I fear is a growing attitude of indifference, a refusal to become involved in the needs and troubles of other people. Indifference is one of the most deadly and killing things one can experience. It is unlikely that Christians in this country will be persecuted and driven into any modern catacombs. What threatens to weaken, if not to destroy, the Church is the bland indifference of some of its members and the increasing callousness of the society in which the Church is set. A burning concern and compassion will have to inspire Christian people if the Church is to make a real impact upon society, and if society is to be delivered from the attitude which says, "I'm all right, Jack," or "I couldn't care less." This is the way of death to the soul.

To continue the parable, we dislike the roughness and pot-holes of the old roads which hasten the depreciation of our streamlined models as we bump across them. They compare so unfavourably with the smooth macadamized surface of the motor highways. But their very pot-holes have a lesson to teach us. It is that we are deluding ourselves if we think that the path of life should always be smooth.

The modern trend is for people to look, as it were, for shock-absorbers to take all the bumps out of life. They want tranquillisers to lull them into a false sense of security. No doubt they will get them if they seek them. Aldous Huxley has pointed out that modern pharmacology can produce drugs which will waft away the effect of most of the ills to which human flesh is heir, at little or no physiological cost. He also makes it clear, however, that it will be equally possible by the same means to make people happy in spite of the fact that they live in sub-human conditions. In either event they will live in illusion, not in reality.

This is not the answer. We cannot cushion ourselves against the hardness of life, because hardness is an essential part of living. As we look to the future we shall be more realistic if we look for ways of coping with life rather than for means of escaping from it. We cannot solve our problems by tranquillisers. When their effect wears off the root of the trouble still remains.

By all means let us look forward to the increasing comforts which modern knowledge can bring us. We can be thankful for the gadgets which make life easier. We no more want to go back to vast, dreary Victorian houses than we wish to continue travelling on pot-holed roads. But life will always have its difficulties, and we must face up to them. It is the good way, of which Jeremiah spoke, which gives rest to our souls. The spurious tranquillity of drugs will not satisfy us. We need the peace which comes through struggle and achievement, and we cannot have it apart from Christ.

The Church faces no easy task in the future, but it has something which the world cannot do without. It has Jesus Christ, who is the same yesterday, today and forever. He covers past, present and future. Every age sees new facets of His truth. We have not exhausted the unsearchable riches of Christ. Indeed it would sometimes seem as if we have done little more than scrape their surface. Certainly this is true of one's own life as an individual. There always seems to be so much more that one could have done, and so much more still to do.

I believe this is also true of the Church. There may be times when we feel despondent about it, but we are never despairing, because it is not *our* Church but Christ's. I think I should have to despair of the future if I were a humanist. The final epitaph on the humanist's position was written by Ovid when he said, "I see and approve better things, but follow worse." How different a spirit that is from the words of St. Paul to the struggling little Christian community at Corinth when he wrote, "I shall remain at Ephesus until Whitsuntide, for a great opportunity has opened for effective work, and there is much opposition."

I believe that the situation for the Church today remains the same. There is much opposition, but a great opportunity for effective work. In the final chapter of this book I shall attempt to say something about the part which the Church has to play as it faces the road ahead, following in the footsteps of Him who is the way, the truth and the life.

12

OPPOSITION AND OPPORTUNITY

"THE part which the Church has to play as it faces the road ahead. . . ." Having written those words I then began to wonder if I had bitten off more than I could chew. After all, this was a vast subject. I could write as only a grass-roots parish minister. Anything I had to say was bound to be limited. Perhaps it would have been wiser to leave such a large question alone rather than deal with it inadequately. I began to have misgivings.

These misgivings were considerably increased a fortnight later, when I found myself in hospital, recovering from a heart attack. Indeed I felt thoroughly humiliated. What a climax to the writing of a book called *Coping With Life!* What right had I to advise others when I had failed to cope with life myself? I had always thought that I was strong and healthy, but here I was, flat on my back, not allowed even to wash my own face! How, I said to myself, are the mighty fallen!

When the first shock had passed, however, I began to see things more clearly. I had known for some time that I had been trying to do too much. I had even made plans to do less, but the heart attack had come before I could put them into operation. It became very clear to me that I should be exceedingly thankful. I had not been given a knock-out blow. The doctors told me that if I took care and obeyed orders I should be able to do my normal work again. It was as if, out of the blue, I had been given a word of warning; as if someone had said to me, "It's high time that you were at the receiving end and began to sort out your priorities for living."

I have always felt that there is a danger of speaking in too easy or familiar a way about the interest which God has in us as individuals. I am embarrassed when over-earnest Christians talk about our Lord as if He were the chap next door. And yet I believe, as I have said earlier in this book, that the purpose and providence of God work even in our insignificant lives. For that reason I could almost welcome the experience of illness, if only because it allowed me to test for myself the kind of advice I had often enough given to others. Here was apparent opposition to my plans, in that I was compelled for some time to be inactive. Was there an opportunity in the opposition?

It seemed to me, as the days passed, that there was. I had always told hospital patients that their illness could be a worthwhile experience. I began to find how true this was for myself. What I had not realised was the therapeutic effect of being in a large and busy hospital ward. There are, of course, minor irritations, but in my experience they are more than offset by the advantages of being in constant touch with other people.

There is little chance of brooding over one's own ills when there are so many others who have more to bear. Further, to anyone who is interested in human nature a hospital ward provides a rich variety of characters. At one moment I would find myself talking with John about the best way of dealing with his alcoholism. At another I would be laughing till the tears came, as Bill described the day when he had missed the chance of £100,000 by making one fatal alteration in the fair copy of his football coupon. Fred, I confess, shook me when he informed me that I should never work again; but I began to understand him better as he told me about himself. His trouble was that his wife had to go out and work for him; and there were times, he said, when the shame of it made him weep like a child.

Three weeks in hospital taught me a great deal. Perhaps most of all I learned to be thankful. Thankful for the skill of the doctors and the care of the nurses; thankful for the extraordinary kindness of so many friends, and for the awareness of their thoughts and prayers; thankful for having been taught a lesson and having been given the opportunity to make a fresh start; thankful, in one word, to God.

So I felt that I could still say something about coping with life, and that I might even try to say something about the Church. True, I should have to write from the viewpoint of a parish minister limited by the experience of the congregations in which he had served; but that might not be a complete disadvantage. After all, a good deal of the New Testament derived from the life and activity of local congregations. The early Church began with small gatherings of believers in Ephesus, Philippi, Corinth and Rome. They met with a good deal of opposition, but they never failed to look for opportunities. They contrived to be the spearhead of the Church's impact upon the world. In fact, the Church could never have existed at all, apart from groups of believing, worshipping and serving Christians.

It may be true enough that the average congregation does not present an exciting or even an attractive picture to the beholder. It may be that this has more often than not been the case for close on two thousand years. Yet the Church has survived, and it will continue to survive. Its reality and its enduring power depend not upon its imperfect and unprepossessing members, but upon God. It is God's Church, not our Church. It is the Church which Christ loved and for which He gave Himself, not the Church which we keep alive by our efforts.

Thus one can agree with John Henry Newman when he wrote, "The Church is ever ailing and lingers on in weakness, 'always bearing about in her body the dying of the Lord Jesus that the life also of Jesus might be made manifest in her body.' Religion seems ever expiring, schisms dominant, the light of the Church dim, its adherents scattered. . . . Meanwhile, thus much of comfort do we gain from what has been hitherto—not to despond, not to be dismayed, not to be anxious at the troubles which encompass us. They have ever been; they shall ever be; they are our portion. 'The floods are risen, the floods have lifted up their voices, the floods have lifted up their waves. The waves of the sea are mighty and rage horribly; but yet the Lord, who dwelleth on high, is mightier.'"

This, I am sure, is true. Newman was writing in 1834. He may have been depressed by the state of the Church at that time, but it was on the eve of one of its most spectacular forward movements. The day was dawning when the great missionary expansion of Christianity was going to spread throughout the world.

At the same time, a belief in the survival value of the Church is no excuse for a flabby apathy on the part of its members. I remember an older minister who used to say to me when I raged about congregational indifference, "Ah, my boy, be patient! We must wait for the Holy Spirit to revive us!" I should have been happier to accept his view if I had not had the uneasy feeling that it was less indicative of a longing for the stirring of the Spirit than of a desire to continue in the same easy way to which the years had accustomed him. We must certainly have faith in the Church as a divine institution, but our faith must show itself in the kind of action which sets the human fellowship of the Church aflame.

One thing which my experience of congregational life has taught me is that the Church begins to come alive when it sees opposition as opportunity. I can remember quite clearly when I first realised this. It was on a summer evening in 1934 when I went to Govan Old Parish Church in Glasgow, where George MacLeod was in the midst of his notable parish ministry. On one side of the ancient graveyard stood mean tenement buildings. On the other was the high wall of a shipyard. It was the time of the depression. The shipyards were idle and thousands of men were unemployed in Govan. It would have been all too easy for the Church to stagnate in the doldrums.

As I walked across the graveyard I saw that the doors of the church were open and that a steady stream of people was coming and going. They were lay members of the congregation engaged in a mission to the parish. They had prayed in the church and gone out two by two to visit the homes in the area with a message of friendship. Now they were coming back to report progress. This was a stage in a two-year plan, which was to culminate in a memorable "Week of Friendship" in the autumn of that year.

What was so attractive to a young man like myself was simply the sight of a congregation, under vital and courageous leadership, going into action in this and in many other ways. In a day when the Church seemed ineffective and uninspiring to many, George MacLeod got things done in a local situation. He had the gift of using opposition as opportunity. In a vivid and practical way he showed us that the Church could recapture its missionary purpose in what was becoming a post-Christian era, and that a congregation could be a living and active fellowship. Before this I had found more fellowship in the university rugger team than in the Church. Now I began to see that there was a deeper experience in the life and witness of a Christian congregation than I had met with anywhere else. It was challenging, invigorating, and above all enjoyable.

Thirty years have passed since then. Slowly the pattern of congregational life has begun to change. There is a growing emphasis upon the missionary task of the congregation and upon the part which the laity can play. It is becoming more obvious that sedentary Christians give the Holy Spirit scant opportunity. One begins to feel that the Church might really be on the move again.

There is, of course, a temptation to feel that there are in one's own congregation peculiar difficulties which provide an excuse for inaction. Thus opposition is allowed to block progress. I have known this temptation, but experience has taught me that no situation is so bad that it cannot be improved, under God, by a combination of faith and works.

When I was called to North Leith Parish Church in 1942, the outlook did not seem hopeful. The church had been damaged by a land-mine. The congregation were divided and dispirited. They were in debt to the tune of several hundred pounds. Their total givings to the wider work of the Church of Scotland amounted to £19. If I had thought only of these obstacles and my own inadequacy we might have made little progress. As it was, the years I spent in North Leith were among the hardest and the happiest I have known.

In any such situation one is driven to depend on God and other people. It was obvious that as a congregation we should have to find our unity in working as a team for a worthwhile end, and in overcoming obstacles together. Two fields of activity were ready at hand. One was the damaged building, which had to be restored. The other was the parish area, which had been allowed to lie fallow.

There is always resistance to change, and there was considerable opposition to the bold plan which our architect, Ian Lindsay, outlined for the renovation. It combined respect for the original Georgian design with the introduction of light and colour to an interior overlaid with gloomy Victorian decoration. It also involved the removal of the organ from behind the pulpit to the west gallery. This proposal roused many to righteous wrath, which was scarcely mollified when I pointed out that in 1888, five hundred members of the congregation had organised a petition against any organ at all being placed behind the pulpit. With a struggle, plans were passed, but many good folk viewed them with considerable misgivings. So the restoration was postponed, which, in the event, was providential.

In the meantime we embarked on a parish mission. It had a salutary effect, both upon the fellowship of the congregation and as a means of bringing new people in. Just as the mission was reaching its climax the roof of the church began to collapse. This was really an excellent thing, although it did not seem so at the time. It gave us something to work for.

It created an atmosphere of crisis; and there is nothing like a crisis for pulling the best out of people.

In truth the task we faced seemed formidable. Not only was the roof collapsing, but the whole building was also riddled with dry rot, from the steeple to the undercroft. Fungi were growing out of the plaster on the walls. Water poured through the ceiling. Sometimes I would go to the scene of desolation at night, listen to the rain dripping down, smell the decay and wonder how on earth we should ever raise the money to pay for all the repairs. The opposition seemed unduly strong. As new ravages of rot were discovered the target figure doubled and trebled. It was hard to remember the opportunity.

Within two years, however, we were back in our renovated church, lovely in its simplicity, light and colour, with every penny paid. This was done by a congregation with no moneyed magnate behind them. It was the result of the team-work of a fellowship who, by their response, rebuked me for my lack of faith and strengthened my belief in the untapped resources which are waiting to be used in every congregation.

I found this to be just as true, if in another way, in my present charge. No two congregations are alike, and the problems of the old parish church of Dundee were quite different from those of an industrial parish like North Leith where the bulk of the membership lived near to, and found much of their social life in the church. In St. Mary's the people were scattered all over the city, and there was little social activity on the church premises.

There was also, I found, a prevailing impression in Dundee that St. Mary's was an exclusive congregation, composed of fashionable, upper-middle-class people; that it was impossible to obtain a sitting in a pew; and that in any event strangers were unwelcome.

All this was a caricature of the truth. The membership was, in fact, a complete cross-section of the population, with as many industrial workers as professional and business people. The members were most friendly and kind, and had a real affection for their church. They did, however, cling to the unfortunate custom of reserved sittings. This undoubtedly helped to present the wrong "image" of the church to any outsider. It made an excellent excuse for anyone who did not attend church to say "I can't get a sitting" or "I am nervous about taking someone else's seat." It helped to build up the picture of the church as a cold, unfriendly place.

This, of course, is merely a local example of a general problem, which is that the Church is regarded as being a predominantly middle-class institution. It is taken for granted that large numbers of the so-called working class who came into being after the Industrial Revolution have never belonged to the Church. There is some truth in this view, but in the old parish churches of Scotland there has always been, both in the country and in the industrial areas, a broad representation of every stratum in society. The trouble has been to fuse them into a living fellowship which transcends the barriers of accent, dress, education, home and income. This is a demanding challenge which is not found in congregations (whether suburban, industrial or in housing estates) where people come from the same social background. It is also vitally important (and not least in an age of social revolution) that the Church should be a truly class-less society; and that is one reason why I have been thankful for the opportunity of serving in a charge like St. Mary's.

Part of the answer, we discovered, lay for us in Christian Stewardship. Once we embarked on our Stewardship Campaign, the erstwhile thorny issue of reserved sittings was swept away. We simply abolished them, and they were never missed. We found that volunteers sprang up for all kinds of jobs, and from every section of the congregation. People met and worked with each other who had never known that they went to the same church. There was a new eagerness to welcome strangers, which was noticed by visitors who came to services. Resources of leadership were brought out in the laity, who bore practically the whole brunt of the work. There was a new sense of fellowship.

This was particularly noticeable at the congregational supper, where 1,200 of us met together for a common meal. To it came one old-age pensioner who lived by herself in a humble little house. She was scarcely fit to come, because she suffered from a cancer of the face which was in its last stages, but she struggled out to join us. Afterwards, when she was dying, she said to me, "It was a wonderful night. We were just one big, happy family."

The process still continues. We know that we are only at the beginning, that there is a long way to go and that we have much to learn. The one thing we are certain of is that the pattern of our congregational life is changing. We must go forward; we cannot go back. We must look on opposition as opportunity.

So much for the parochial experience of an individual. There are, however, broader issues which affect all members of the Christian Church. It seemed to me that rather than range too widely in these final pages I might turn to the early Church for guidance and example. Having quoted St. Paul's words about the opposition and opportunity which he found at Ephesus, I read again in Acts 19 the account of his ministry there. I felt that in many ways the situation then was similar to that which the Church faces today.

When Paul arrived at Ephesus he found some Christian converts there already. At once he said to them, "Did you receive the Holy Spirit when you became believers?" "No," they replied, "we have not even heard that there is a Holy Spirit." Their only experience was of the baptism of John for repentance. They knew nothing about the baptism of Jesus with the Holy Spirit and with fire.

When Paul looked at these people he must have seen that there was something missing in them. It sounds as if he could tell by their very appearance that they had not received the Holy Spirit. This made me think of a railway journey in India on the way home from Australia. My wife and I were travelling with Duncan Fraser, one of our Scottish missionaries in Bombay. At one of the halts we were walking along the platform, and the guard spoke to him in Marathi. I asked Duncan if he knew the man. "No," he replied, "but I knew, when I saw him, that he was a Christian. You can spot them by their faces."

In the same way Matthew Roydon wrote of what he saw in Sir Philip Sidney:

> *A sweet, attractive kind of grace,*
> *A full assurance given by looks,*
> *Continual comfort in a face,*
> *The lineaments of Gospel books.*

Here are the marks of the Lord Jesus, the signs of the Holy Spirit. That we should show them in our lives matters more than all our writing and our speaking. It is by our being and our doing that we shall make plain what Christianity means. Perhaps we can too often give the impression that we have not even heard that there is a Holy Spirit. But the Holy Spirit has not changed, nor have men and women. It is for us to make the contact so that we can express in our lives (and show in our faces) what we believe in our hearts.

There is much more both to warn and encourage us in St. Paul's ministry at Ephesus. As usual he began with the synagogue, the established Church of his day. He did his best with the official custodians of religion, but they would have none of him.

He had come up against the opposition of reactionary conservatism, in the basic sense of refusal to budge from an entrenched position. It was the new wine and the old wineskins all over again. He gave the Jews of the synagogue three months, and then he gave them up.

The Church runs the risk in every age of being like the synagogue. There are always elements in it which are solidified in complacency, smug and inward-looking, repellent to the outsiders and infuriating to many who would love to see the Church bold and venturesome. It is almost too easy sometimes to draw a parallel between the organized Church and the synagogue, to lose oneself in a welter of destructive criticism, to cry that the Church is finished and that something else must take its place.

Yet this is no solution. True, St. Paul left the synagogue; but the Church, for all its faults, is not in the same category. The real reformers never stop at destructive criticism. They always have a constructive policy which wins support at least from the bolder spirits. They never seek to sweep away the Church and replace it by splinter groups. They take the difficult way of following the light which is given to them within the Church, in the faith that the Holy Spirit does lead into all truth. What St. Paul did was not to sweep away the heritage of the past but to use it to build on for the future.

So in the Church we can never be static. We must combine two qualities, permanence and change. We must show that we reflect the life of Jesus Who is not only the same yesterday, today and for ever, but Who also says "Behold! I am making all things new!"

The Church must also speak in a language which ordinary people can understand. Too often in sermons or in speeches at Church Assemblies it seems as if the Church is talking to itself. It was different with St. Paul. Having left the synagogue, he held daily meetings and discussions for two years in a lecture hall. He must have got his message across to the people, for his reputation spread throughout Asia Minor. As with Jesus, "the mass of the people listened eagerly to him".

It is, of course, much easier for the Church to preach to the faithful than to interest the sceptics. It is a pity that many theological discussions, which are so fascinating to the participants, are often incomprehensible to anyone else. Ironically enough, a great deal of such theology is centred round the teaching of the man who spoke so clearly to the ordinary folk in Ephesus. There is no real need for theology to be clouded by technical jargon or for intelligence to be equated with obscurity. The Church's message has to be taught with clarity.

This is all the more necessary when one considers the growing opposition of the sects today. At Ephesus St. Paul had to deal with travelling exorcists who claimed the name of Jesus. Today the name of Jesus is claimed by bodies like the Mormons and Jehovah's Witnesses. The growth of these movements illustrates the Church's failure to educate its members. The sects gain their converts not from the ranks of the unbelievers but from lapsed, indifferent and uninstructed Christians. The strange inconsequences of Joseph Smith and Judge Rutherford carry no weight with those who know the essentials of the Faith.

The sects batten upon the failures of the Church. Their members are also imbued with a sense of urgency which springs from their conviction that everyone but themselves will go to hell. The fact that the Mormon heaven will have no room for Jehovah's Witnesses makes little difference to either body. Over against such enthusiastic certainty (however mistaken) the invincible ignorance and Laodicean lukewarmness of some Church members have no defence. It is high time that the Church saw more clearly in the opposition of the sects the opportunity for a revival of Christian education.

Above all, the Church has to see the opportunity of making an impact upon the life of the community and society in which it is set. Undoubtedly one of the potent reasons which kept St. Paul at Ephesus was the exciting effect which Christianity was having upon the city. There had been a sharp decline in idol worship and a marked fall in the sale of the silver shrines of Diana. The livelihood of the silversmiths, said Demetrius, was threatened; and when he added that the high standard of living of the citizens was in danger there was an immediate uproar. Christianity had made its impact.

It seems to be a general view that any effect which the

Church has upon society today is weakening, because of the decline of religion. If this is so, there is all the more reason for those who hold strong Christian convictions to let them be heard. It may well be a healthy sign when Christians provoke opposition. Missionaries are often criticised for "educating the natives" and "giving them ideas above their station". Such criticism springs from a desire to maintain a high standard of living based on exploitation. It shows that Christianity has hit the mark. Similarly there are those who dislike Christians standing up for the rights of minorities, or who object to the opposition shown by the Church to the imposition of Central African Federation against the will of the people, or who say that it should not become involved in the *apartheid* struggle in South Africa. Those who make such objections would seem to be deaf to the echoes of Ephesus, and to forget that Christianity is in essence revolutionary.

To be sure, the average Sunday congregation does not seem to present a revolutionary appearance. And yet what a tremendous potential it has, and what an impact it can make through its members on the life of the community in which it is set.

Take, as an example, a congregation like my own. In it there are members of the Town Council, lecturers in the university, teachers in schools. There are doctors, lawyers and accountants. There are business men and factory owners, shipyard workers and weavers in the mills. There are members of the Chamber of Commerce and shop stewards, bankers and labourers, personnel officers and professional footballers, students and journalists—a glorious mixture, with infinite possibilities. And such a congregation is only an infinitesimal fraction of the whole Church, the Body of Christ, throughout the world. The potential influence is immense, the actual effect far greater than we may imagine.

The years I have spent in the parish ministry have convinced me that while we may be depressed at times about the Church we should never be despairing. We can prove for ourselves that Christ makes all the difference in our own lives. Nothing can shake us in that conviction. We can also discover that no situation is so bad that we cannot, with God's help, make it better. We can see with our own eyes the advance that can be made in the life and work of local congregations and in the progress of Christian causes all over the world.

Why should we ever fear for the Church? It is "the Church of the living God, the pillar and bulwark of the truth". If there is anything shoddy or untrue in the Church we can be sure that it will not endure. It will be eliminated. Thus the apparent weakness of the Church can be the sign of its purging and preparation for greater tests. The Church is not finished, nor are its great days past. Perhaps its full glory is yet to be seen. In the meantime it is for us to persevere in the Church, knowing that it contains the truth about human nature, the truth about right human relationships and the truth about God's plan for redeeming His rebellious children so that they may live in harmony with Him and with each other.